Naoshi Yamawaki

Glocal Public Philosophy

Philosophy in International Context
Philosophie im internationalen Kontext

edited by/herausgegeben von

Hans Lenk

in connection with:
Ioanna Kuçuradi, Matthias Maring, Herta Nagl-Docekal,
Gregor S. Paul, Hans Poser, William Sweet, Tran Van Doan

Volume/Band 9

LIT

Naoshi Yamawaki

Glocal Public Philosophy

Toward Peaceful and Just Societies in the Age of Globalization

LIT

Bibliographic information published by the Deutsche Nationalbibliothek
The Deutsche Nationalbibliothek lists this publication in the Deutsche Nationalbibliografie; detailed bibliographic data are available on the Internet at http://dnb.d-nb.de.

ISBN 978-3-643-90291-7

A catalogue record for this book is available from the British Library

Klosbachstr. 107
CH-8032 Zürich
Tel. +41 (0) 44-251 75 05 Fax +41 (0) 44-251 75 06
E-Mail: zuerich@lit-verlag.ch http://www.lit-verlag.ch

Distribution:

In the UK: Global Book Marketing, e-mail: mo@centralbooks.com
In North America: International Specialized Book Services, e-mail: orders@isbs.com
In Germany: LIT Verlag Fresnostr. 2, D-48159 Münster
Tel. +49 (0) 2 51-620 32 22, Fax +49 (0) 2 51-922 60 99, E-mail: vertrieb@lit-verlag.de
In Austria: Medienlogistik Pichler-ÖBZ, e-mail: mlo@medien-logistik.at
e-books are available at www.litwebshop.de

Contents

Preface and Acknowledgements

After the end of the Cold War, we entered the era of unstable globalization. Against the optimistic view of Francis Fukuyama, who thought that world history had come to an end with the conclusion of the Cold War and that there would be no great conflicts in the future,[1] we have experienced many monumental, tragic historical events since then. These include the Yugoslav Civil War; the terror attacks in New York on September 11, 2001; the unjust Iraq War; the world financial crisis; the great disaster in Japan on March 11, 2011; the recent Civil War in Syria; the emergence of ISIS; and so on. How can philosophy contribute to the change for the better in this catastrophic situation? This is a very difficult and serious question. Nevertheless, philosophers have to try to answer this question from a different viewpoint than that of politicians.

I have been engaged in the interregional philosophical dialogue organized by UNESCO since 2004. This dialogue has been aimed at removing Eurocentrism and rediscovering or creating philosophies based upon the characteristics of each region in order to overcome any conflicts due to ignorance of different cultures. In this sense, it was a project against Huntington's view of "The Clash of Civilizations."[2] Unfortunately, this project seems to have been interrupted now, but I firmly believe that it should continue; albeit on a small scale. Indeed, this book is just a small outcome of my philosophical thinking about the topic during the last fifteen years.

Since the 1990s, the slogan "Think Globally, Act Locally" has become widely favored; especially in NGOs. I am in favor of this practical slogan; however, a new coinage, *glocal*, began to be used by Japanese private enterprises in particular, and its meaning is somewhat ambiguous and arbitrary. The adjective *glocal* in the title of this book, *Glocal Public Philosophy*, has, however, a clear philosophical meaning; i.e., the global character of a particular world or place where each individual lives and acts. *Glocal Public Philosophy* is therefore a practical philosophy that deals with "universal public issues from the particular public world or place where each individual lives and acts." I have tried to develop this idea in

1 See Fukuyama [2006/1990].

2 See Huntington [1996].

view of contemporary philosophies both in Western countries and in Japan as far as possible.

To facilitate readers' understanding, I would like to mention the composition of this book. Chapter 1 provides an introductory overview of the contents of the following chapters. The main points here are historical changes to the nature of public philosophy, as well as academic situations, from the 19th century onwards, and the necessary ideas to break through such situations. The idea of *glocal* public philosophy as a trans-national public philosophy, together with a new ethics, will be put forward here. Chapter 2 lays a philosophical foundation for this idea in view of contemporary Western philosophies, while Chapter 3 offers a critical consideration of the positive and negative legacies of public philosophies in modern Japan since the 1930s. Chapter 4 focuses on the historical development of ideas on Democracy and Civil Society in Japan, enabling us to reflect on the past and make future efforts to develop trans-national democracy and civil society based on the *glocal* public philosophy. Here, I compare the development of ideas of civil society in Japan to that in Germany, because the modern history of both countries shares a similarity pre-WWI and a big difference post-WWII. Chapter 5 treats the serious theme of the orientation of philosophy after the great disaster on March 11, 2011. In my view, what has been missing in the theory of modernity in Western philosophies is the problem of nuclear power as a result of the progress of science and technology; therefore, we have to newly orient philosophy and ethics to overcome the modern crisis produced by it. The final chapter focuses on the idea of *WA* for world peace, which I have been developing on the occasion of UNESCO conferences. When expressing the Japanese proper name in these chapters, I write the family name first and the given name after (as is customary in Japanese).

I hope the readers of this book can begin to read any chapter according to each interest. Throughout the book, I shall be extremely happy if the reader can obtain not only new knowledge about modern Japanese public philosophies but also inspiration to consider the new role of philosophy for the realization of more peaceful and just societies (as indicated in the subtitle).

I would like to express my gratitude to various persons for the publication of this book. First of all, I thank In-Suk Cha, professor emeritus at Seoul University, for recommending that my manuscript appear in the series "Philosophy in International Context" (Lit Verlag); Professor Hans Lenk for adopting my manuscripts in this series; and Dr. Michael J. Rainer at LIT Verlag for kindly advising on their publication. Second, I would like to thank Luca Maria Scarantino, professor at the IULM University and General Editor of the scholarly journal *Diogenes*, for giving me the chance to edit the special issues on "Japanese Philosophy Today" (Volume 57, Number 227) of *Diogenes* for Sage Publishing, in which I was able to develop my own idea of *glocal* public philosophy. I am also grateful to Mr. Hattori Eiji, Former Advisor to Director General of UNESCO, and Non-profit Kyoto Forum Foundation, for giving me the chance to develop my own ideas on *WA* and other matters. I would like to thank several scholars in Europe, especially Klaus Mainzer, a prominent professor at the Technological University of Munich and the President of the German-Japanese Association for Integrative Science, for developing my idea on the holistic view of knowledge and learning. I would also like to thank Gesine Foljanty-Jost, professor emeritus at the university of Halle-Wittenberg, for developing my thinking about the idea of civil society, and Alain-Marc Rieu, professor emeritus at Jean Moulin University Lyon 3, for developing my ideas on modernity.

Lastly, I express special gratitude to Inoue Hajime, the president and chair of Seisa University, for financial support, and Dr. Lucinda Ireson for the thorough correction of my English.

1 Introductory Overview – Toward a Trans-National Public Philosophy as Comprehensive Trans-discipline for the 21st Century*

In this introductory chapter, I will present a historical overview of key concepts that will be addressed in this book, such as public philosophy in general and, in particular, academic situations, trans-disciplines, and trans-national public philosophy, as well as public ethics and *glocal* public philosophy.

1.1 The Concept of Public Philosophy in General

The term "public philosophy" appears to have come into usage in the 20th century; especially in the English-speaking world.[1] If, however, we define the concept of public philosophy as "the philosophy, in which the various public issues such as political legitimacy, social justice, war and peace, environmental problems, public memory etc. are philosophically discussed," equivalent concepts can be found in the classics of Western as well as East Asian countries. Indeed, its long tradition dates back more than 2,000 years. For example, Aristotelian practical philosophy, which was put forward in ancient Greece and which consists of ethics, politics, and rhetoric, could be regarded as the origin of public philosophy in Western countries (Aristotle [1996], [2000]). Aristotelian practical philosophy has been influential in the Arabian medieval age, as well as the European world, and is now considered to be the origin of republican public philosophy. On the other hand, it is the Confucian philosophy represented by Confucius and Mencius that could be regarded as the origin of East Asian public philosophy. This East Asian tradition was transformed into the Neo-Confucian philosophy in medieval China by Zhu-xi as well

* This chapter is a slightly modified version of my previous article: Yamawaki [2010].

1 See Lippmann [1989/1955], Bellah et al. [1985] pp.297-307, and Sandel [2005]. In Japanese academia, independent of the English-speaking world, there has been interdisciplinary exploration and dialogue on public philosophy since the 2000s, which could be called an academic movement and in which a number of innovative research projects were completed. The academia in China, too, has gradually become familiar with the new academic concept of Public Philosophy. In June 2009, thanks to the efforts of Prof. Meimao Lin at Renmin University of China, the People's Publishing House published a translation series of 10 volumes of "Public Philosophy," introducing the latest research results from Japan.

as Wang Yang-ming, and it exerted much influence on Japanese and Korean public philosophy in the pre-modern era.

These traditions were transformed in modern Europe. The social contract political theory represented by Hobbes, Locke, Rousseau, and Kant, the economic theory represented by Smith, Malthus, and Marx, and the sociological theory represented by Comte, Spencer, Durkheim, and others appeared one after another. These theories were almost literally imported into East Asian countries, especially modern Japan, from the end of 19th century onwards, and they began to compete with one another.

Moreover, it must be pointed out that modern socio-political, as well as academic, situations since the 19th century are characterized by the following two aspects:

1. The transformation of public philosophies from *cosmopolitan to nationalistic* on a socio-political level.
2. The transformation of the relationship between *philosophy and social theories* on an academic level.

Clarifying such situations, this paper aims to conceive trans-national public philosophy as a comprehensive trans-discipline for the 21st century.

First, I will review the traits of public philosophies since the 19th century on a sociopolitical level in Europe and Japan. Then, I will review the transformation of academic situations in general from the 19th century until now. After that, I will try to advance trans-national public philosophy as a comprehensive trans-discipline for the 21st century, which consists of the new public ethics and *glocal* public philosophy, together with new understandings of Self, Others, and the Public World.

1.2 The Traits of Public Philosophies since the 19th Century on a Socio-political Level in Europe and Japan

I would like to begin by reviewing the traits of public philosophies since the 19th century on a socio-political level in both Europe and Japan.

As is well known, Kantian public philosophical works such as *What is Enlightenment* and *To Perpetual Peace* (written in the late 18th century) were not intended for a particular nation but for the world citizen. Indeed, Kant's idea of "public use of reason" was conceived as an indispensable right of the world citizen, and his idea of "public orders" consisted of not only the national and international level but also the world citizen level (Kant [1964, 1970/1785], [1970, 1972/1795]). In this sense, Kant can be called a *cosmopolitan* public philosopher.

The development of public philosophies began, however, to feature more and more nationalistic traits in Western countries from the 19th century onwards. As a matter of fact, Fichte, who regarded himself as the genuine successor of Kant's transcendental philosophy, advocated a closed trade state and unification of the German people as one nation in order to resist Napoleon's imperialism. Approaching this from the public-philosophical concept of the Self, the Kantian *cosmopolitan Self* was replaced in Fichte by a *national Self*, which has to be generated through national education and culture (Fichte [1978/1808]). In this sense, Fichte can be called a *nationalistic* public philosopher.

In the case of Hegel, the matter is a little more complicated because he thought that not only the national Self but also the *European Self* played the most important role in the public space. Hegel tried to describe the new modern Europe changed by the French revolution, as well as the industrial revolution, in a comprehensive way in his *Philosophy of Rights* (1821). He rejected Kantian cosmopolitanism as illusionary and regarded the constitutional sovereign state, which was supposed to be legitimized by the mutual recognition of the people's freedom and excellent government officials, as the most important public institution (Hegel [1970/1821]). In contrast to Fichte, however, Hegel attached much importance to world history, which was recognized as the progress of the consciousness of freedom among the people. By the people, he meant merely the European people, because it was only they who knew the value of freedom. As for the Asian people, he despised them for their ignorance of freedom (Hegel [1970/1840]). This view of world history and world culture in Hegel is in sharp contrast to that of Leibniz, who, as a cosmopolitan philosopher in the late 17th century and the early 18th century, emphasized various individuals (monads) in the world and highly appreciated the Chinese intellectual culture of his day.[2] Thus, Hegel became a representative of *Eurocentric public philosophy* that had not really been seen before the 19th century.

After Hegel died, the constitutional national state system in Europe developed gradually but in a conflicting way, as was seen in the relationship between France and Germany. This conflict culminated in WWI breaking out in 1914, which also rendered the leftist internationalism illusionary. That is, the Marxian belief that the proletariat has no national border was betrayed by the fact that so many laborers preferred their national identities to their international identities in this historical catastrophe.

What is noteworthy about this situation in terms of public philosophy is that an American journalist, Walter Lippmann, published an epoch-making book and criticized the manipulation and stereotype of public opinion on the basis of his experience during WWI. According to him, the people were manipulated in the pseudo-environment made up by the media, becoming akin to the mass-like prisoners in the cave that Plato had once criticized. In this regard, the public as an important actor of democracy is nothing but a phantom (Lippmann [1987/1922], [1993/1925]). To this end, it is well known that John Dewey presented a counter-

2 On this topic, see Perkins [2007].

argument with the intention of rehabilitating the public (Dewey [1954/1927]). I shall discuss the contemporary relevance of this issue at the end of this chapter, as well as in Chapter 2.

Now, I will review the traits of public philosophies in modern Japan.

As is widely recognized, Japan's modernization began with the *Meiji Renovation* in 1868, when the new emperor replaced the Tokugawa shogunate, the feudal status was abolished, and the new construction of an integrated national polity started. It should be stressed that this renovation was not a coup d'état; rather, it was a quasi-revolution by the corporation of upper and lower samurai who wished to change the Japanese system as a whole and to cope with Western great powers since the 1850s. In this process, I would like to direct attention to a Neo-Confucian public philosopher who exercised an intellectual influence on this movement; i.e., Yokoi Shōnan (横井小楠 1809-1869).

After Commodore Matthew Perry of the United States arrived in Japan suddenly in 1853, there was a hot debate between samurai on whether to open the country and trade with foreign countries or to battle with foreigners and maintain national isolation. Then, Shōnan converted from the latter position to the former based upon a Neo-Confucian thought: the *Universal Public Principle (Logos) of Heaven and Earth* (天地公共の実理). According to him, this principle has a universal or transversal validity in distinguishing between decent and indecent countries. On an international level, Shōnan approved of opening Japan to foreign countries, because America and other Western countries could be regarded as more decent than Japan. On the domestic level, he considered that the ultimate legitimacy of politics lies in the public discussion of the Japanese people (公論、公議) and that Japan should become a more virtuous country through this dialog. His quasi-cosmopolitan thought changed, however, and he placed increasing stress on the importance of national defense after he became conscious of the danger of the state egoism of Western countries.[3]

As a matter of fact, public philosophies in the *Meiji Era* (since 1868) had been closely connected with nationalism. For Fukuzawa Yukichi (福沢諭吉 1834-1901), for example, who could be regarded as one of Japan's representative modern public philosophers, it was most important to build the Japanese nation from each private person. He declared that there is only a government and no nation in Japan, and he thought that the foundation of the Japanese nation should be realized by the power of individuals who absorbed the learning (Fukuzawa [1963/1872-76]). In this regard, his *national and liberal* public philosophy has been considered a positive example to be realized by the Japanese people until now.

---

3 It is only recently that Yokoi Shōnan has begun to be reinterpreted as a very important public philosopher in early modern Japan. See Minamoto [2005]. An old view that sees Yokoi as a cultural imperialist, as represented by Sansom [1962 p. 269], must now be rejected.

From an international perspective, however, Fukuzawa's public philosophy, as characterized in the slogan he advocated in 1885 after the breakdown of the revolutionary project led by Kim Ok-Kyun (金玉均) in Korea – "Let's leave Asia (for Europe 脱亜論)" – was very ironic, because the Europe of this time knew no substantial public space beyond the limits of each nation-state. In fact, Fukuzawa intended to establish a state-sovereignty in Japan that would be just as strong as that seen in European powers (Fukuzawa [1973/1875] Chap. 10). He showed, at least after 1885, little interest in other Asian countries and much more interest in the promotion of Japanese power. Consequently, his thoughts on enlightenment did not offer the Japanese people any critical viewpoint against the colonialist behavior of the Japanese state in China from 1895 and in Korea from 1910.[4]

Thanks to the Anglo-Japanese Alliance (1902-22), Japan in the *Taisho Era* (1912-26) could share the victory of the First World War with other great powers. It must not be forgotten, however, that Taisho Democracy developed in the context of *imperial* Japan, for Japan in those days had possessed colonial control of Taiwan since 1895 and Korea since 1910. Japan was really an empire in East Asia at that point. On the domestic level, the important political outcomes of Taisho Democracy were the founding of the Party Cabinet in 1918 and the establishment of universal male suffrage in 1925.

The most famous public philosopher in this era was Yoshino Sakuzo (吉野作造 1878-1933) at the University of Tokyo, who was a Christian and quasi-Hegelian thinker. In 1916, he advocated the idea of constitutional politics and political systems "rooted in the people" (民本主義 *Minponshugi*) instead of the term of democracy (民主主義 *Minshushugi*), which could be associated with Rousseau's theory of general will. According to him, the former is compatible with both monarchism and the republic, while the latter is compatible only with the republic. Similar to Hegel's abovementioned *Philosophy of Rights*, Yoshino attached much importance to the role of professional policy makers such as governmental officials and political parties entrusted by the Japanese people.

On the international level too, Yoshino, who universalized a Hegelian view of history, considered the victory of Japan over Russia, along with the revolution of China in 1911, as a victory of freedom over despotism. He studied the modern history of China intensively, focusing especially on revolutions, and even tried to vindicate the protest movement of the Chinese students against feudalism and Japanese imperialism, which broke out on 4 May 1919, because it aimed for freedom and *Minponshugi* (民本主義).[5]

Regarding Japanese colonial policy in Korea since 1910, Yoshino was not so

4 Regarding recent studies on this theme, see Schad-Seifert [2003].

5 Unfortunately, Yoshino's works are not yet translated into English. However, two excellent studies about him in English by Najita [1974] and Stegewerns [2003] deserve mention here.

radical as to assert to aim to abolish it, and, indeed, that was obviously one of his limits, but he was very critical of the assimilation policy in those days, which ignored the cultural identity of the Korean nation.

As for views on the relationship to Asia during this time period, there were a few Japanese thinkers such as Miyazaki Toten (宮崎滔天 1871-1922), who advocated solidarity against Western colonialism with revolutionary China and were admired by Yoshino (Miyazaki [1982/1902]) and others. Still, they exercised minimal influence on the Japanese nation. Instead, the ultra-nationalistic tendency grew in increments to such an extent that the Japanese government established the puppet-state of Manchukuo and allied with Nazi Germany. In this situation, nothing was as deceptive as the ideology of "The Greater East Asia Co-Prosperity Sphere (大東亜共栄圏)" put forward by the Japanese government in 1940, because the reality in East Asia was by no means of a co-prosperous nature. Rather, it was merely imperialistic in nature, as evidenced by the policy through which Japan forced East Asian people to speak Japanese in their countries' schools. In addition, the ideology of "Overcoming Modernity" (that is, overcoming Western individualism, liberalism, and capitalism, as advocated by some Japanese intellectuals in 1942), was based on total negligence of the imperialistic behavior of Japan in Asian countries.[6] I will discuss these problems in detail more philosophically in Chapter 3 and more historically in Chapter 4.

In this context, I feel obliged to mention one first-class Japanese scholar on Islam: Ōkawa Shumei (大川周明、 1886-1957). Indeed, it is only through Ōkawa that Islamic philosophies were introduced to modern Japan. He translated the Koran into Japanese and published an introductory book about Islam. Unfortunately, however, he was so captured by nationalism that his sympathy with Asian thought and antipathy to Western colonialism did not lead him to solidarity with other Asian people but to a Japan-centric expansionism. As a result, he was charged with war crimes after WWII. It is a great pity that he could not develop his knowledge on Islam in a more cosmopolitan manner.[7]

If we here consider the situation of Western Europe after WWII, we can see that it has changed greatly. The nightmare and trauma of two World Wars forced European statesmen and people, particularly in Germany and France, to construct a public space that would go beyond the level of nation-state. Though the future of the EU remains to be seen, the transformation of *national into transnational public space* continues to take place in Europe today.

By contrast, such a transformation is not evident in East Asian countries. On the political level, the key problem lies within the postwar Japanese government,

---

6 On this theme, see Calichman [2008]. Still, the author seems to overestimate the influence of this wartime event on current Japanese politics and culture.

7 On Okawa, see Szpilman [1998].

which made it a rule to follow the international policies of the United States of America uncritically. Japanese intellectuals in WWII are likewise not without their faults, as they focused on the modernization of the individual as a nation and did not attach much importance to the problems of overcoming the history of modern Japan in Asia. It is thus an apt time to develop *trans-national public philosophy* in East Asia; especially because the relationship between Japan and China or Korea has not improved even 70 years after World War II. I will take up this problem again in Chapter 4.

1.3 The Transformation of Academic Situations from the 19th Century until Now

Now, I will review the transformation of the academic situation since the 19th century.

To begin with, I would like to introduce an overview of developments in social theory and philosophy since the beginning of the 19th century, dividing these into the following three periods:[8]

1. *The period of pre-specialization* in the social sciences, when philosophy sought to unite and contain all sciences within itself, as exemplified by German idealism from Kant to Hegel. Hegel's *Encyclopaedia of the Philosophical Sciences*, written for his lectures at the Humboldt University of Berlin in the 1820s, can be regarded as a typical example of the integrative philosophy of this period.
2. *The period of specialization*, when the separation of the social sciences from philosophy took place while specialization within the sciences continued. Max Weber's lecture *Science as a Vocation* (1919), which declared specialization to be the destiny of the time, is regarded as the classic view of science from this period.
3. *The period of post-specialization*, when the relationship between the sciences, including technology and philosophy (and incorporating ethics), is becoming closer again and may well characterize the scientific situation for the 21st century. This is the background against which I would like to develop trans-disciplinary, as well as trans-national, public philosophy.

I will now explain this scheme in detail.

To understand the great transformation of the academic situation in the 19th century, it is advisable to begin with the comprehensive concept of philosophy in

8 I first introduced this historical perspective of Wissenschaft in terms of the categories of pre-specialization, specialization, and post-specialization in my book (Yamawaki [1999]), and, since then, I have been emphasizing it in a number of my books and papers in order to highlight the historical particularity of our contemporary environment of social sciences. See also Yamawaki [2009].

so-called German idealism as a classical paradigm of philosophy, which characterizes the *period of pre-specialization* in the social sciences. Indeed, despite their metaphysical differences, the representative philosophers in this movement held a common idea that all sciences could obtain their validities through the philosophical foundation. Therefore, they regarded philosophy not as a discipline but as a trans-discipline that lays the foundation for all sciences.

Whether Kant belongs to German idealism or not, it is certain that his new idea of the faculty of philosophy pursued by free-minded scholars in isolation from that of theology, law, and medicine provided an impetus to think about the location of philosophy in the university (Kant [1959/1798]). In fact, Schelling's famous book on the method of academic studies, published in 1803, stressed that philosophy could not be institutionalized as a specific discipline but should be learned as a fundamental science in a free association of all faculty members (Schelling [1974/1802]). This idea exerted a great influence on Wilhelm von Humboldt, who founded Berlin University. However, Schelling did not develop his theory of sciences any more after he had shifted his philosophical interest from the sciences to human evil and religion. Accordingly, we can hardly find any public philosophical social theory in his writings.

Unlike Schelling, Hegel retained his interest in the systematic theory of the sciences until his death. He regarded philosophy as the total system of philosophically-founded knowledge, which consisted of logic, natural philosophy, and the humanities (Hegel [1998-99/1830]). As is evidenced in his declaration that "philosophy is its time grasped in thought," it was especially important for Hegel to develop the philosophical system with regard to the new social and academic situation in the Europe of his day [1970/1821]. As a matter of fact, his system of humanities contained anthropology, phenomenology, psychology, philosophy of rights, philosophy of arts, philosophy of religion, etc. It must be emphasized here that the Hegelian system is related closely to his theory of the development of the human subject who acquires knowledge through the process of both alienation and realization. Hegel's public philosophy as presented mainly in his *Philosophy of Rights* also presupposed a theory such as *Phenomenology of Mind* [1952/1807].

This philosophical system was, however, characterized by Hegel's Eurocentric thought, as pointed out in the previous section. Moreover, it assumed the concept of absolute knowledge, which meant the ultimate place and viewpoint of totality for the human subject to reach [ibid. § 8]. Because such a concept was anticipated in Hegel's philosophy, it left an impression of a closed system and collapsed after his death.

The academic situation after Hegel's death can be called *the period of specialization of the sciences*, while the Hegelian system was representative of *the period of pre-specialization*. In fact, philosophy lost its intellectual power to integrate the sciences, and many sciences became more and more independent of philosophy from the middle of the 19th century to the middle of the 20th century. The faculty or department of natural sciences separated itself from philosophical sciences, and new faculties or departments such as political science, economics, and sociology have arisen as special disciplines. In parallel, philosophy fell into a crisis of identity and was degraded to a special discipline. Social theories too, which had a long tradition from Plato and Aristotle to Hegel and not only described social realities but pursued ideal visions of society, were de-philosophized and split into several discrete disciplines such as sociology, economics, political science, and cultural anthropology. As the most representative theorist of social sciences in this period, I would now like to address M. Weber's view of science.

Regarding the theory of science, Weber indeed owed a lot to Neo-Kantians such as H. Rickert or W. Windelband in that he regarded social science as a cultural science, which relates to the understanding of values. Weber emphasized, however, the distinction between social scientific knowledge and value judgments. He declared namely that an empirical social science cannot tell individuals what they *should* do but rather what they *can* do. Value judgments are a matter of personal individual decision based upon each person's worldview, while social scientific knowledge belongs to the sphere of academic research based upon what Weber calls "ideal-types" (Weber [1968a/1904]). At the end of his essay "Objectivity" in 1904, Weber attached much importance to the value-consciousness of each scholar in the age of specialization of the sciences and suggested that the understanding of the sciences could be changed in the future (ibid. p. 213). He also criticized the specialist without spirit in the last part of his *Protestant Ethic* in 1905 (Weber [1963/1905] p. 204).

Nevertheless, this viewpoint seems to have faded away in his extremely popular book *Science as a Vocation* in 1919. In this book, Weber regards his contemporary academic situation as the stage of specialization, which has never been seen before but will continue in the future. In his view, philosophical ideals such as the "way to the true being, way to true art, way to true nature, and way to the true God etc." cannot be justified anymore, because a new time of polytheism of values has begun. What is important in such a situation is that intellectuals understand and endure it so as to serve special disciplines as their vocations. The question of the ultimate meaning of science does not belong to science but to the decision of every person who leads their life in their own way. The social sciences can teach people how to understand political, economical, and social phenomena by means of ideal types, but they can never provide an answer to the question of whether such phenomena are worthy of existence.[9] With this dualism of scientific validity on the

9 I have been stating this critical opinion on Weber's view of the sciences, which is still influential on social scientists, both in Japanese and English. See Yamawaki [2007].

one hand and meaning of life on the other, Weber limited the role of philosophy to taking a stance in the everyday life of each individual (Weber [1968b/1919a]).

I appreciate Weber's theory of social sciences in the *period of specialization*, as well as just after WWI, insofar as it warned us against an obsolete presumption that philosophy can integrate the social sciences in a speculative way, as German idealism had once tried. However, I have to say that his view of social science, which had been influential on the social sciences and existential philosophy in the 20th century, is obsolete today.

The main reason why I believe this is that normative political and social theory, which Weber (apart from his theory of power politics) excluded from the social sciences and hardly conceived, began to be strongly rehabilitated from the 1970s onwards. By this, I mean the normative political theory developed by J. Rawls [1971], M. Walzer [1983], C. Taylor [1994], and M. Nussbaum [2006], the normative economic theory developed by A. Sen [2000], the normative social theory developed by J. Habermas [1981], and others. These currencies can be called a *nouvelle vague* of public philosophies, because they have been discussing normative public issues such as justice, wellbeing, human development, multicultural public space, democracy, etc., in both theoretical and practical ways. In fact, these public issues could not be discussed without value judgements, which Weber had denied. As a matter of fact, this *nouvelle vague* has been so influential in the academic world that the relationship between the social sciences and philosophy, including ethics, is becoming closer again. Moreover, the radical change of international situations since the 1990s is requiring more and more interdisciplinary cooperation. I would like to call this new academic situation *the period of post-specialization*.

In this *period of post-specialization*, philosophy can no longer remain a separate academic discipline focused solely on the study of earlier philosophies but should be considered a trans-discipline of other disciplines. As a matter of course, arrogant notions such as Hegel's absolute knowledge in the *period of pre-specialization* must be rejected and, instead, philosophy should play an intermediary role and facilitate communication among the various social sciences, including political science, economics, sociology, ecology, and history. It should do this from the perspective of the new public ethics and ontology under the name *glocal public philosophy*,[10] which I will advance at the end of this chapter and in the following chapters.

[10] The following section of this chapter is an abridged version of the theses in my book *Glocal Public Philosophy: A Vision of Good Societies for the 21st Century* (in Japanese). See Yamawaki [2008].

1.4 A New Trans-national Public Ethics for the 21st Century

I will begin to advocate the new *trans-national public ethics*, which covers various dimensions.

First of all, the new trans-national public ethics should develop both against the notorious Samuel Huntington's concept of the "clash of civilizations" (Huntington [1996]), along with a cultural relativism that has no interest in normative ethics, the relationship between the diversity of cultures, or trans-cultural public values. What is especially important here are our efforts to *make mutual understanding of the diversity of cultures in the world compatible with trans-cultural public values such as peace, wellbeing, human rights, etc*. Certainly, there are distinct kinds of cultures and religions in the world, and it is wrong to abandon trying to understand them; let alone agitating the clash of civilizations. In fact, it is not civilizations but ignorance of them that brings about such a clash. The new ethics excludes any cultural imperialism that assumes one culture surpasses others, as was seen in Hegel (mentioned above).

At the same time, the new trans-national public ethics attaches much importance to *trans-cultural* public values such as peace, wellbeing, and human rights, because they provide the preconditions for human beings in any cultures to lead good lives. In this regard, it criticizes any ethnocentrism that denies such trans-cultural public values. To sum up, the new public ethics holds the view that the understanding of human beings cannot be separated from the context of the different cultures in which each individual lives, and, because of that, both cross-cultural dialogue and trans-cultural public values should be promoted.

This ethical thinking about cultures necessarily relates to the new *public ethics about history*. It was a great mistake to assume that this history ended with the termination of the Cold War, as Francis Fukuyama once thought with reference to Hegel (Fukuyama [2006]). On the contrary, we entered a new historical stage in which various conflicts caused by historical events were revealed and needed to be solved. This is the chief reason why we need a new ethics of history that requires dialogue between the past, present, and future, as E.H. Carr advocated (Carr [1964/1961] pp. 123-124). However, the new public ethics for the 21st century cannot take over the quasi-Hegelian progressive viewpoint clearly found in Carr, who seems to have believed in the progress of world history. Ideology such as "Cunning of Reason" (in German, *List der Vernunft*) in Hegel or "Historical Necessity" in Marxism can no longer be adoptable to explain the past. Instead, non-Euro-centric viewpoints have to be taken into consideration.

The new trans-national public ethics on history is characterized by how it considers modern history not only from *positive viewpoints* such as emancipation of peoples from oppression, the building of a constitutional state, etc., but also from *negative viewpoints* such as the arrogance of cultural imperialism, barbarous acts of modern sovereign states, suppression of one people by other people, religious intolerance, etc. This ethics makes efforts to eliminate such negative elements in history as far as possible. I will now develop this ethical thinking based on concrete examples.

As shown in the second section above, the history of public space since the 19th century has been closely connected with nation-state building and colonialism. Therefore, each characteristic of nation-state building differed from one another; even in Asian countries. For instance, Chinese nation-state building was combined with resistance against imperialistic invasion by Western countries, as well as by Japan. The Indian people, Arabian people, and African people have other great histories in their nation-state building. By contrast, the Japanese nation-state was related to imperialistic behavior that caused great damage to Korea, as well as China. It should be a serious task and intergenerational responsibility for the Japanese to overcome negative legacies of modern history such as colonialism. In any event, each different consciousness of modern history should adopt a different stance on the *intergenerational responsibility for the positive, as well as negative, legacy of the past*. Only then will we be able to undertake common intergenerational responsibilities for the future.

In this regard, we need the idea of what South African public theologian John De Gruchy calls 'restorative justice' (De Gruchy [2002]). This idea stands in contrast to notions of retaliatory justice such as 'an eye for eye; a tooth for a tooth.' The restorative justice aims not at revenge but at apology and forgiveness.

I might incidentally remark that restorative justice has a different feature from the distributive justice that has been discussed recently by Rawls [1971], Walzer [1983], and others, because the former takes on a historical-temporal character. It requires us to admit the undeniable historical facts and errors of the past, to co-memorize them in the present, and to have a strong will to overcome the past and construct common values in the future. Without such historical and temporal elements, there can be no restorative justice. The *public world involves not only the spatial-present dimension but the temporal-historical dimension*. Therefore, it would become a great challenge for trans-national public ethics to deal with the past, present, and future of a public world in which human beings live based upon restorative justice.

The process of reconciliation is not, however, a masochistic one as some people mistakenly assume. In my view, *reconciliation is not the ultimate end but a necessary condition for realizing co-happiness among the various peoples who live in various cultures*. That is why we need intergenerational responsiveness for our public-common future.

In this regard, I have to introduce cosmopolitan ethics in the sense that we have a responsibility to take on a *positive legacy of cultural resources* in the world. Indeed, using or studying cultural resources as important public goods must not be confined to particular peoples or nations but rather spread all over the world. Still, because there are different languages and cultures in the world, it would be natural for each ethical subject that has both universality and cultural particularity to adjust this responsiveness according to individual situation, tradition, and ability. Fortunately, there are a few common cultural resources in East Asian countries such as Chinese characters or script, Confucianism, and Buddhism, and it would be a great task for the East Asian people to reconstruct (or deconstruct) their positive legacy for future generations.

Intergenerational responsiveness, as well as responsibility for the future, would be more clearly recognized were we to consider our future in a more comprehensive and interrelated perspective, tackling global issues such as ecology and environment, economic development, education, world peace, human rights, and so on. We would not be able to deal with these issues without regard to future generations. To reinforce this point, I will propose here a new *ethics of public (common) good/bad.*

The notion of public (or common) good is predominantly treated from a perspective of institutions, and this is regarded as a concept encompassing material objects and systems. Thus, public good includes not only moral good but also social good. As founders of the ethics of public good, which should be differentiated from virtue ethics, Thomas Aquinas and Friedrich Schleiermacher should be mentioned. Aquinas regarded "society" (in Latin, *societas*) as human activity with the aim of realizing "the good life, including material welfare."[11] In his doctrine, Schleiermacher investigated "a totality of goods, which results from the organization and institutionalization of reason," citing scientific communities, states, voluntary social organizations, and churches as concrete examples.[12]

According to a remarkable report by the *United Nations Development Programme*, global public goods must fulfill the minimum criteria of offering "benefits to more than two states" and providing "benefits that are strongly universal in terms of countries, people, and generations." These global public goods are then classified in accordance with three more specific concepts; namely "natural global commons" such as the ozone layer, atmosphere, and climate; "human-made global commons" such as norms and principles accepted worldwide (e.g., universal human rights), scientific knowledge, the internet, etc.; and "global policy outcomes" including peace, health, and stable financial markets (Kaul, Inge, et al. [1999] pp.454-455). *Trans-national public ethics* must now take on the role of

11 On the contemporary relevance of the common good theory of Aquinas, see Keys [2008].

12 In my view, the legacy of Schleiermacher's ethics should be more appreciated by contemporary scholars. See Schleiermacher [2002/1812-17].

providing the ethical basis for the concept of global public goods as trans-national public values.

This ethics must also study the antithetical concept in this regard; namely, public bads, which can then serve as the basis for *global* public bads. The United Nations Development Programme focuses on the following "global public bads": depletion of the ozone layer and increased levels of radiation, the risk of global warming, violation of human rights, injustice, lack of equal rights, exclusion and inequality of access in regard to information, wars and conflict, epidemics, and financial crises, among others. Ways should be found to rectify these problems on a trans-national basis (ibid.). A typical example of these "global public bads" is the financial crisis, which occurred in 1997 and 2008. This must be considered from the new perspective of trans-national public ethics.

1.5 A Short Comment on Peace as a Trans-national Public Value

In connection with the previous section, I, as a Japanese scholar, will now make a short comment on peace as a transversal public value of great importance. The *Preamble to the Japanese Constitution* that was promulgated in 1947 declares as follows:

> We, the Japanese people, desire peace for all time and are deeply conscious of the high ideals controlling human relationship and we have determined to preserve our security and existence, trusting in the justice and faith of the peace-loving peoples of the world. We desire to occupy an honored place in an international society striving for the preservation of peace, and the banishment of tyranny and slavery, oppression and intolerance for all time from the earth. We recognize that all peoples of the world have the right to live in peace, free from fear and want.
>
> (http://www.solon.org/Constitutions/Japan/English/english-Constitution.html)

I think this is a particularly important declaration that includes trans-national public values such as world peace and justice.

Roughly speaking, there are two concepts of peace: *negative peace* and *positive peace*. *Negative peace* means the absence of overt violent conflict. We can see this concept in Hobbes' theory of Leviathan. To escape from the state of nature characterized as "bellum omnium contra omnes," Hobbes advocated that we should make by our mutual contract 'Leviathan,' which secures our peace and safety (Hobbes [1958/1651]). In my view, this Hobbesian idea has not yet lost its actuality. Far from it: when we glance at places such as Iraq and Palestine, it is evident to many that Hobbesian theory is applicable. In this sense, there is no denying the value of negative peace.

Nevertheless, it must be pointed out that the people under the control of a Leviathan can have only the right to live safely, the right to reject involvement in a life-threatening war, and the right to maintain silence under arrest. Any other human rights such as the freedom of speech, expression, and academic thought cannot always be guaranteed under Leviathan. Furthermore, a Leviathan is based upon the fear of state authority, as well as upon a distrust of human nature.

On the other hand, *positive peace* means a state where peoples have collaborative and supportive relationships. With respect to European social philosophy, this concept of peace was defined clearly by Spinoza, who said that "peace is not the mere absence of war, but a virtue based on strength of mind." According to him, the Hobbesian thought "bellum omnium contra omnes" would be realized insofar as the human being is subordinated to the passive mind (passion). The human being is, however, able to obtain the active mind by intuition, intellect, and intellectual love of God (=Nature) (Spinoza [1958]). It is this active mind that creates positive peace.

Spinoza conceived the best state (commonwealth) as one in which the people live in harmony. Such a state is established by free people, who are led more by hope than by fear, whereas conquered people are led more by fear than by hope. The former (hope) seeks to improve life; the latter (fear) seeks only to avoid death (ibid. p.311). It is clear that Spinoza's conception of positive peace addressed a wider view of human rights than Hobbes' Leviathan.

From a contemporary perspective, the notion of *positive peace* has been strongly advocated by Johan Galtung. He defines positive peace as the state in which there is no *structural violence*. Structural violence denotes a form of violence that corresponds with the systematic ways in which a given social structure or institution kills people slowly by preventing them from meeting their basic needs. Institutionalized racism, sexism, elitism, and ethnocentrism are examples of this. Positive peace cannot be realized without eliminating such structural violence; in other words, without realizing human rights in the sense of both economic rights, social cultural rights, and civil and political rights, as the *International Covenants on Human Rights* declares (Galtung [1996]).

While *negative peace* does not always relate to social justice as another public value, *positive peace* always relates to the idea of social justice. By global justice, I mean various sorts of justice such as distributive justice, ethno-cultural justice, and environmental justice, which must be discussed together with positive peace and human (economic, social, cultural, civil, political) rights all over the world.

I think, however, that we should go beyond the theory of human rights and social justice in order to realize positive peace. As the famous *Preamble to the UNESCO Constitution* declares, "since wars begin in the minds of men, it is in the minds of men that defenses of peace must be constructed"; that is, we have to deal with the problem of the human mind. In this regard, we could view Spinoza as a pioneer of a philosophical foundation of peace, even if we do not agree with his metaphysical pantheism.

In this respect, I would like to think again about the Japanese term *Heiwa* (平和), which means peace. Literally, the character 平 (Hei) means mild, impartial, horizontal, etc., and the character 和 (Wa) means harmony, softening, mitigating, appeasing, calming, etc. The Japanese people, including me, should not forget the past errors made by Japan in Korea and China, as well as the atomic bombings in Hiroshima and Nagasaki that resulted from US involvement.[13] I will discuss this theme again in the final chapter.

1.6 The Concept of *Glocal* Public Philosophy and a New Understanding of Self, Others, and World as Its Basis

Now, I would like to deal with the theme of what could be called a new ontology for public philosophy in the 21st century.

As treated above, a trans-national public ethics that tackles problems such as world peace, economy, environmental crisis, human securities, and so on requires trans-national cooperation and a *new philosophical understanding of the Self, Others, and Public World*. However, I hesitate to call this kind of trans-national public philosophy a global one for two reasons. First, I hesitate because the name "global public philosophy" is easily associated with mono-culturalism. The adjective "global" seems to me not able to do justice to the diversity of the world. Even if the humanization of globalization is advocated, it still sounds like a prescription for homogenization.

The second reason is a more philosophical one; namely, the problem of the understanding of a Self who talks about global issues. In my view, human beings are always existing in the world (in German, *in-der-Welt-Sein*), as the great philosophers of the 20th century such as Martin Heidegger [1977/27], Maurice Merleau-Ponty [1945], Paul Ricoeur [1969], Charles Taylor [1989], and Kitaro Nishida [1993/1945] emphasized. That is, the Self should be always understood as *a located or situated Self*, and it is of great importance to recognize the situations in which people face or treat global issues such as peace, justice, human rights and securities, environmental crises, and so on.

This is why I think that the name of global philosophy is rather misleading, and I would like to adopt the name of *glocal* public philosophy as my coinage instead so as to overcome the limits of national public philosophy. The adjective "local" means "existing in or belonging to the area where you live, or to the area you are talking about" (see *Cobuild Advanced Learner's English Dictionary, New Digital Edition*). Therefore, *glocal public philosophy can be defined as a trans-*

13 On this theme, see Yamawaki [2006].

national public philosophy, which deals with global issues not from nowhere but from somewhere to be locally characterized. What is important is the correlation between the globality of issues and the historically, as well as culturally, characterized localities in which each human being lives. The global and local viewpoints are seen as interdependent, and public values and particularity of thinking are then viewed as hardly separable.

To reinforce this program, however, a new *theory of Self, Others, and Public World* is needed. Indeed, it is right that Michael Sandel once criticized John Rawls, as Rawls's theory of justice lacks consideration of the problem of the encumbered Self (Sandel [1982]). Still, it is important for a *glocal* public philosophy to develop an ontological foundation in a much more comprehensive way in order to avoid falling into ethnocentrism or irresponsible rootless universalism.

To lay the foundation of the *glocal* public philosophy in an ontological way, I will first introduce the concept of *Cosmopolitan Self as a new dimension of multiple understandings of the Self*. This concept has a long tradition with roots extending to the Stoics, Christianity, and Kant (as mentioned in the first section) in Western countries, and it is also combined with the consciousness of 天 (Ten) in Neo-Confucianism, as well as God in the Muslim world. The Cosmopolitan Self understands himself or herself as a member of the Earth; i.e., a cosmos in which all of humankind lives. The Cosmopolitan Self also understands being in the universalistic way. Still, it must be emphasized that this notion of Cosmopolitan Self must be combined with other public dimensions of understanding of the Self, which are characterized by cultural-historical differences or particularities. In concrete terms, the Self and the world in which he or she lives possesses a unique history depending upon the identity of the person in question; for example, contemporary Japanese, Korean, Chinese, Indian, Arabian, American, African, French, German, and so on. This individual holds the mental responsibility for his or her past and must make efforts to understand Others who live in different cultures and histories. In this respect, *the universalistic viewpoint of Cosmopolitan Self and multicultural viewpoint of Particular Self should not oppose but complement each other*. It should be pointed out that local governments, workplaces, places of worship, schools, universities, and other associations or communities also belong to the public world, which is constituted not only by the nation but by the people who do not belong to the nation. Moreover, multiple understanding of the Self and Others would play a critical role in enabling people to communicate with one another in these various public worlds. I will develop this thought in the following chapters.

I would like finally to take up the issue of a trans-national public. In order to think about this issue, it is prudent to recall the controversy between Lippmann and Dewey, which I mentioned above in the second section; not only because both can be seen as representative public philosophers of the 20th century but because the issue between them about the public as "a set of people in a community who share common interests" seems more and more important in the 21st century. In my view, the main point of dispute between them relates to the rebirth of the public in the Great Society, which can be called the global society in today's terms. Lippmann's post-WWII public philosophy does not concern the public in general but rather public intellectuals, who can criticize mass society, including the mass media and unlimited pursuit of profits, and perform civility as the main actor in the public world (Lippmann [1989/1955]). Dewey's public philosophy, on the other hand, assumes a well-educated public in general, who can perform democracy in the sense of "the mode of associated living" as the main actor in the public world (Dewey [1954/1927].

In my view, these classical views of Lippmann and Dewey seem to have been demonstrated in the recent Iraq War. At the beginning, the majority of the US media offered the people false information about the presence of weapons of mass destruction and helped the Bush administration start an illegal war. I think this is a typical case of what Lippmann once warned. However, it should be remembered that, at the same time, there were very strong anti-war networks and movements formed by internet users all over the world. I regard this phenomenon as what Dewey called Formation of a *Great Community*. Based upon this monumental case, I want to insist that we can and should make Lippmann's realistic viewpoint and Dewey's idealistic viewpoint compatible. *Glocal* public philosophy based upon a new understanding of Self, Others, and Public World takes over Dewey's ideal without forgetting the realistic criticism of manipulation by the mass media. It consequently tries to undertake philosophical and democratic education for all, opposing all fundamentalisms and imperialisms.

2 The Idea and Scope of *Glocal* Public Philosophy from a Comparative Perspective of Western Philosophies

In this chapter, I will expound the idea and scope of *glocal* public philosophy introduced at the last section of the previous chapter. For this purpose, I would like to begin by looking back on representative Western philosophies in the 20th century, which had great influence on the academic world; not only in Europe but in Japan and other Northeast Asian countries. Next, I will appraise several public philosophies in the last one hundred years in Western countries.

Based upon this perspective, I will elaborate the ontological traits of *glocal* public philosophy, which I call *glocal ontology*. Lastly, I will clarify the scope of *glocal* public philosophy in terms of its trans-disciplinary role in learning and social ethics.

2.1 Critical Comments on Representative Western Philosophies in the 20th Century

As described in the previous chapter (1.3), in what I call the *period of pre-specialization* until Hegel, philosophy sought to unite and contain all sciences. In what I call the *period of specialization* after the death of Hegel, however, the separation of the social sciences from philosophy took place, while specialization within the sciences went on. What dominated academic philosophy in this period was the so-called Neo-Kantianism such as the Marburg School, represented by H. Cohen, P. Natorp, and E. Cassirer, and the South-Western School, represented by W. Windelband and H. Rickert.[1]

The Neo-Kantian school attempted primarily to lay a philosophical foundation for the natural sciences and cultural sciences, respectively, from the 1870s to the 1910s. Because of its overly formal thinking, however, it was not especially successful, although it had some influence on famous scholars such as Max Weber, whose notion of social science and of Ideal-type owed much to Rickert's epistemology. As I described in the previous chapter, he limited the role of philosophy to

[1] On this period of philosophy, see Schnädelbach [1984].

take a stance in the everyday life of each individual. In any case, Neo-Kantianism lost its influence on the academic world after the First World War.

In my view, three new currents of philosophy replaced Neo-Kantianism in the 1920s; i.e., a) the *Logical Positivism or Empiricism* represented mainly by the Vienna Circle, b) *Neo-Marxism* represented by G. Lukács or the Critical Theory represented by M. Horkheimer and T. Adorno, and c) *Hermeneutical Ontology* represented by M. Heidegger.

I will now endeavor to make some comments on their traits in my own manner.

2.1.1 Logical Positivism or Empiricism and Critical Rationalism

This current of thought aimed at integrating the sciences under the banner "Unified Science" is based upon the reductionist thesis that all the theories and results of the various sciences can be, or ought to be, expressed in common languages, and that the special sciences share a common method. With this thesis, "Logical Positivism" aimed at making the scientific worldview popular not only among scholars but also in the public life of the people.[2] The most enthusiastic advocate of Unified Science was Otto Neurath, who was also a fervent socialist. He insisted that even the social sciences ought to be studied in physical and behaviorist languages (Neurath, Carnap, Morris [1944]). In later age, he developed a strong interest in the idea of a common language through which to communicate with one another beyond the limit of nations at the global level, and he put forward the idea of an isotype for global politics (Neurath [2011]). In this sense, it could be said he was a quasi-public philosopher.

Further, Neurath advocated an anti-foundational account of knowledge, as illustrated by the following metaphor.

> We are like sailors who on the open sea must reconstruct their ship but are never able to start afresh from the bottom. When a beam is taken away a new one must at once be put there, and for this the rest of the ship is used as support. In this way, by using the old beams and driftwood the ship can be shaped entirely anew, but only by gradual reconstruction.[3]

This phrase was popularized by American philosopher W.V.O. Quine in his book *Word and Object* (Quine [1960]). The quasi-holistic view of science endorsed by Neurath was doomed to failure, however, because it retained an emphasis on physicalism and, curiously, went against his holism, thus entailing a kind of reductionism.

After World War II, the "Ordinary Language School" represented by the later Wittgenstein, Austin, and others, on the one hand, and "Critical Rationalism" represented by K. Popper, on the other hand, became influential as offshoots of Log-

---

2 For an introductory overview of logical positivism, see Kraft [1968]

3 See Neurath [1921].

ical Empiricism. While the Ordinary Language School was mainly interested in the philosophical analysis of ordinary languages but hardly in social or public philosophy,[4] Critical Rationalism had been interested in the public character of knowledge on the basis of open society, as well as the open mind of each scientist. Popper advocated piecemeal social engineering for solving social problems under the slogan "ought implies can." To be sure, this current offers us a very important method for empirical social research and social policy (Popper [1957]). I would like to adopt this idea in my own method, as described in the fourth section of this chapter. Still, this concept had no interest in any normative theory about justice, human rights, etc., because it strongly rejected the essentialist approach of social science or theory. It is an irreversible achievement that this current overcame the weakness of Logical Empiricism. I have to say, however, that it did not develop any productive public philosophy due to its lack of a normative theory.[5]

2.1.2 Neo-Marxism and Critical Theory

These currents of thought were advanced by G. Lukács and M. Horkheimer in the 1920s, respectively.

In his impactful book *Geschichte und Klassenbewußtsein*, published in 1923, Lukács criticized Neo-Kantianism because it could not understand the total reality of human life. He insisted instead that only Marxian philosophy is capable of grasping the total reality. Moreover, he dared to say that it is the proletarian classes that can break the deadlock of social situations in Western countries. His new concept of "Neo-Marxian philosophy" consisted of not only Marx's view of humankind but also of German idealism; especially Fichte's active philosophy (Lukács [2013/1923]). This reformulation was successful among certain leftist intellectuals but was too romantic to grasp the total reality of human life. Therefore, Lukács himself modified his thought gradually and became more and more dogmatic (Lukács [1954]).

"Critical Theory" appeared in the 1920s and was developed in the 1930s at the University of Frankfurt. That is why Critical Theory is also called "the Frankfurt School." It attempted to understand capitalist society both totally and critically, and it took a clear stance against both contemporary positivism and anachronistic metaphysics. The adjective "Critical" in this school does not mean limitation in a Kantian sense but rather criticism of society in a Marxian sense (Horkheimer [1992/1937]). Differing from orthodox Marxism, however, Critical Theory adopted not only a Marxian critique of capitalist society but also a Freudian critique of culture. More originally, Horkheimer and another representa-

4 Even exceptional social philosophies from the perspective of analytical philosophy such as Winch [1958] and von Wright [1971] cannot be deemed public philosophy in this sense.

5 On this criticism, see my dissertation, Yamawaki [1983].

tive of Critical Theory, T. Adorno, wrote *Dialectic of Enlightenment* in the 1940s and described the fate of modern instrumental reason that had led to Auschwitz (Adorno and Horkheimer [1969/1947]).

Their attempt was indeed successful in criticizing authoritarian society during and after World War II. Their influence did not last long, however; especially because Critical Theory lacked a normative theory of society in the positive sense. Though Adorno's "Negative Dialectic" could offer a critical viewpoint against mass culture (Adorno [1973]) and capitalist society, and though Horkheimer's reappraisal of Schopenhauer (Horkheimer [1981/1960]) suggested "an ethics of solidarity" for suffering peoples, this theory could not offer a positive vision for a just and peaceful society. It was for this exact reason that J. Habermas, the most excellent disciple of Horkheimer and Adorno, left Critical Theory in the 1970s in favor of his own normative theory of society based upon "the communicative actions of citizens in the public space."[6] I will treat the characteristics of his public philosophy in the next section and other parts of this book.

2.1.3 Hermeneutical Ontology

The current of thought represented by M. Heidegger in his major work, *Sein und Zeit* (*Being and Time*) in 1927 offered quite a different viewpoint and dealt with the meaning of Being in the world (in German, *in-der-Welt-sein*). Heidegger introduced his original concept of *Dasein* who interprets the meaning of Self-being, as well as the meaning of the world into which *Dasein* is thrown. *Dasein* is the historical being who knows its mortality and is open to possibilities through commitment to the future. Heidegger, however, regarded the meaning of the public sphere or publicness (in German, *Öffentlichkeit*) in the negative sense as a false way of being (in German, *das Man*) (Heidegger [1977/1927] § 27). Therefore, it lacks the viewpoint of mediation between the historical being and the public sphere in the positive sense. As a matter of fact, Heidegger committed himself once in Nazi Germany and failed. Moreover, he supported the Nazis in a latter half of the 1930s, as his *Black Note* shows (Heidegger [2014]). After WWII, he had not been interested in social ethics, and his former disciple Hans Jonas criticized him harshly in this respect.[7]

In my view, it was one of his disciples, H. G. Gadamer, who developed a positive legacy of *Sein und Zeit* as part of his hermeneutical philosophy. In his monumental work, *Wahrheit und Methode* (*Truth and Method*), published in 1960, Gadamer introduced a new concept of "historically effected consciousness" (in German, *wirkungusgeschichtliches Bewußtsein*). With this concept, he formulated the idea that the understanding of a text means the fusion of horizons thorough

---

6 See Habermas [1981].

7 Jonas' sharp criticism of his former teacher Heidegger; see Jonas [2003].

dialogs between the text and its interpreter, who is embedded in a different historical and cultural context from that of the text itself (Gadamer [1960]). Indeed, Gadamer's great achievement was to develop a new type of mutual understanding, not only of various texts and traditions but also of human beings who live in different cultural and historical contexts, without falling into relativism.

However, Gadamer was not so interested in social or public philosophy that deals with public issues, though his idea of hermeneutics exerted much influence on public philosophers such as Charles Taylor and others.[8] In my view, it was Hannah Arendt who started from Heidegger's philosophy and developed the new idea of publicness or the public area as a human condition. According to Arendt in her famous 1958 book *The Human Condition*, the term "public" signifies two closely interrelated but not altogether identical phenomena: "It means, first, that everything that appears in public can be seen and heard by everybody and has the widest possible publicity ... Second, [it] signifies the world itself, in so far as it is common to all of us and distinguished from our privately owned place in it" (Arendt [1958] pp. 50-52).

I do not enter into details of Arendt's concept of publicness directly here. Instead, I will reflect on the various public philosophies of the 20th century; including that of Arendt.

2.2 Appraisals of Public Philosophers of the 20th Century

As I declared at the beginning of the previous chapter, the long tradition of public philosophy dates back more than 2,000 years since Aristotelian practical philosophy and Confucian philosophy. However, the name of public philosophy itself in the 20th century was developed mainly in the English-speaking world; especially in the US. The explicit advocates of this name were and are Walter Lippmann, Robert Bellah, Michael Sandel, Robert Goodin [1995]), James Tully [2008], and others. Even so, the philosophers who reformulated the *idea of the public sphere* in the 20th century such as John Dewey, John Rawls, Michael Walzer, Alasdair MacIntyre, Hannah Arendt, and Jürgen Habermas could be called public philosophers, too. From this perspective, I reflect on the public philosophies of the past hundred years in the English and German-speaking world, pointing out the necessity of advancing a *glocal* public philosophy for the 21st century

2.2.1 Walter Lippmann and John Dewey – Mass Media and the Public

I begin by appraising Lippmann and Dewy as the first two public philosophers of the 20th century.

---

8 Taylor [2011] declares that his way of understanding of cultures owes much to Gadamer.

a) Lippmann

I have already mentioned the importance of the famous American journalist Walter Lippmann at the end of the previous chapter. Now, I reevaluate him in the context of public philosophy. In my view, his main achievements as a public philosopher may be reevaluated in two aspects: his critique of mass media and his rehabilitation of civility.

His epoch-making book *Public Opinion*, published in 1922, aimed to criticize the manipulation of the people in the pseudo-environment made by the mass media through the stereotype of images and thinking (Lippmann [1987/1922]). His next book, *The Phantom Public* (1925), pointed out the information gap between the insiders and outsiders in terms of important political affairs and declared that the public as an important actor of democracy had become a phantom (Lippmann [1993/1925]). Looking back at history, this diagnosis, in spite of Dewey's criticism, was terribly accurate and increased its actuality since the 1930s. As a matter of fact, the manipulation of the people by the mass media was so furious that Göbbels' propaganda film instigated the genocide of Jewish people in Nazi Germany, while the Japanese totalitarian system mobilized the whole country by means of stereotypes such as American and British devils. Moreover, Stalinist systems such as those of the USSR, Red China, and North Korea made many propaganda films and spread the myth that socialist countries offered paradise.

After World War II, Lippmann modified his negative view of the public and advanced his own idea of public philosophy so that the US and liberal countries could cope with socialist countries. He subsequently introduced the concept of civility that the citizens in liberal countries must learn. According to Lippmann, freedom of speech is not the end in itself but is a means for the seeking the truth as the end. If it is taken for the end, speech will fall into mere rhetoric or propaganda. Even the property rights of citizens must be regarded as limited in view of the finitude of resources in the world (Lippmann [1989/1955]). The idea expressed by Lippmann in the 1950s thus stood under the influence of classical political and social thought such as the natural Law of Stoics and Thomas Aquinas rather than modern liberal thinkers.

To be sure, Lippmann's idea of public philosophy retains elitist traits that do not pay sufficient attention to the unjust problems in US, which became a great issue in the 1960s. Nevertheless, in my view, Lippmann's public philosophy should be reappraised in that it continually warns us to be careful of the *manipulation of public opinion by the mass media* and not to forget the importance of *civility as a civic virtue*. As a matter of fact, it increases its significance more and more in the unstable age of globalization in which the mass and social media play a very important role. Therefore, we should not underestimate or forget these warnings in the Age of Internet Society, although Lippmann's elitist position should be modified in favor of a more democratic public philosophy.

b) Dewey

As I described in the previous chapter, it was John Dewey who presented a counter-view to Lippmann's critique of the public in the 1920s. Dewey, who experienced student movements such as *The May Fourth Movement in China*, 1919, believed in the well-educated public in general, which can not only perform democracy in the sense of "the mode of associated living" as the main actor in the public world but also reduce the obstacles to democratic society. According to Dewey, the ideas of liberty, equality, and solidarity that were advanced in the French Revolution must be innovated by the *Great Community* among the public in the Great Society. He thought that the local activity of the public and its networks would become more and more important in establishing the Great Community (Dewey [1954/1927]).

From a historical perspective, however, this rather optimistic idea expressed by Dewey in 1927 could not counteract the catastrophic situations since the *Great Depression* in 1929, and it consequently lost its actuality. Indeed, Dewey's idealism was criticized by not only leftist thinkers but also radical theologians such as Reinhold Niebuhr.[9] Nevertheless, Dewey's public philosophy must be re-appreciated today; not only as a forerunner of the communitarians but also as the model of an original public intellectual who offers us the *importance of public communication and education*. Indeed, it will become more and more important to create the *Great Community of the trans-national public* both on the global and local level through a social network in the unstable age of globalization.

2.2.2 John Rawls – A Just and Well-Ordered Society

As I suggested above, the situation in the US changed greatly in the 1960s. The civil rights movement for radical equality in the US, especially against racial segregation in the South, was manifested through nonviolent protest, while popular protest against the Vietnam War became increasingly strong. It is against this background that John Rawls' epoch-making book *A Theory of Justice* appeared in 1971.

As is widely known in the academic world, the aim of this book was to advance a liberal and democratic theory of justice against utilitarianism, which regards the principle of "the greatest happiness of the greatest number" as the notion of justice. According to Rawls, this utilitarian notion must be replaced by the following two principles of justice, which would be agreed as a consensus among citizens who live under the veil of ignorance:

9 On Niebuhr's criticism of Dewey, see Rice [1993].

> Each person is to have an equal right to the most extensive basic liberty compatible with a similar liberty for others. Social and economic inequalities are to be arranged so that they are both (a) reasonably expected to be to everyone's advantage, and (b) attached to positions and office open to all.

These principles are to be arranged in a serial order, with the first principle prior to the second. The distribution of wealth and income (2-b) must be consistent with both the liberties of equal citizenship and equality of opportunity. According to Rawls, this idea of justice as fairness makes it possible to realize a just and well-ordered society. The nature of the Self that corresponds to this idea is a free and equal moral person (Rawls [1971] pp. 54-117).

Since the 1980s, however, Rawls has modified his idea and declared his stance as *political liberalism*, which is distinct from moral as well as metaphysical liberalism (Rawls [2005/1993]). He emphasized then the role of "public reason," which consists of governmental officials such as judges, Diet members, executives, and others. This rather narrow concept of public reason now plays an important role in building the overlapping consensus about the above-stated concept of justice. Although Rawls attaches importance to the reciprocity between governmental officials and ordinary citizens, he excludes *civil society* from public reason and regards its culture only as a background culture to the political forums. In my view, however, this modification seems more of a regression than a form of progress in terms of public philosophy.

Apart from that, meanwhile, radical Rawlsians such as Thomas Pogge and Charles Beitz advocated that distributive justice in the Rawlsian sense should be applied on a global level.[10] In his later years, however, Rawls denied this idea on the grounds that the liberal theory of justice should be restricted in liberal societies and, instead, *the Law of Peoples* that requires the cooperation between liberal societies and illiberal but decent hierarchical societies must be conceived for the stability of international relations. Rawls called this stance "Realistic Utopia" (Rawls [1999] § 1 pp. 11-23).

Thus, in my view, it is a great achievement that Rawls offered a *starting point to rehabilitate the normative political or social theory*, which Max Weber had once denied. What I miss in Rawlsian normative theory is a richer *ontological concept of the Self,* which Rawls intentionally neglected under the name of political liberalism, as well as a richer concept of the *Public World* than that which he assumes.

---

[10] See Pogge [2002] and Beitz [1979].

2.2.3 Amartya Sen and Martha Nussbaum – The Capability Approach

Independent of Rawls, another idea of social justice based upon the so-called capability approach has been developed by Amartya Sen and Martha Nussbaum.

a) Amartya Sen

Sen, a great economist as well as moral philosopher from India, seems to have tried to overcome the weakness of Rawls via his own concept of *capabilities and their functionings*. According to Sen, the concept of *functionings* reflects the various things a person may value doing or being. The valued *functionings* may vary from elementary ones, such as being adequately nourished and free from avoidable diseases, to complex activities or personal states, such as being able to take part in the life of a community and having self-respect. A person's capability refers to the alternative combinations of *functionings* that are feasible for him or her to achieve and, thus, a kind of freedom (Sen [1995]).

Based upon this idea, Sen regards development as a momentous engagement with freedom's possibilities and sees poverty as the "deprivation of human capabilities," which means deprivation of both civil-political rights and economic-social rights (Sen [2000]). He seems, however, to not be interested in the concept of Self, as his book *Reason before Identity* [1999] shows. Consequently, his approach leans on overly abstract and general ideas. For all that, I will support his idea of *human securities and human development* and quote it positively in Chapter 5.

b) Martha Nussbaum

On the other hand, Martha Nussbaum, who has been collaborating with Sen as a prominent philosopher, has tried to develop his theory and has listed the *central human capabilities* as follows: 1) life 2) bodily health 3) bodily integrity 4) senses, imaginations, and thought 5) emotions 6) practical reason 7) affiliation 8) other species 9) play 10) control over one's environment on the political as well as material level (Nussbaum [2000] pp. 78-79). Although this list has been controversial among scholars and even criticized because of its quasi-essentialist nature, it is remarkable that Nussbaum thinks that this approach can overcome the ambiguity of the concept of human rights. According to her, capabilities cover the terrain occupied by both political and civil liberties and economic and social rights. Capabilities also provide an account of extremely important fundamental entitlement that can be used as a basis both for constitutional thought within a nation and for thinking about international justice (Nussbaum [2006]).

Nussbaum regards herself as a cosmopolitan American and therefore seems to agree with the idea of a *Cosmopolitan Self* (Nussbaum [1996]). I greatly appreciate her in this respect. It is somewhat of a pity, however, that she does not deepen the idea of the *Particular Self* as an American and the *Public World* in view of contemporary international situations more ontologically.

2.2.4 The Communitarians – The Self, Social Goods, and Civic Virtue

It is necessary here to take up the traits of the so-called communitarians in the English-speaking world, because they offered several important ideas for *glocal* public philosophy. Against Rawls' view of society, so-called communitarians such as Michael Sandel, Michael Walzer, Alasdair MacIntyre, Robert Bellah, and others emerged in the 1980s. They criticized the right-based theory of Rawls and instead stressed the significance of the *Self, social goods, and civic virtue in the community*. While Rawls emphasized the right prior to the good, communitarians advocated the "priority of the good to the right."

a) Sandel and Walzer

As I pointed out in the previous chapter, Sandel criticized Rawls because his idea of justice presupposes the Kantian Self, which is too abstract and too unencumbered for one to commit oneself to political communities. For Sandel, what matters in political theory is the "Encumbered Self" who takes responsibility for common good in the community in which he or she lives. Without the conception of good life in the community, the theory of justice would be vain. In this sense, Sandel tries to rehabilitate the public philosophy of republicanism based upon civic virtue and common good instead of a liberal public philosophy based mainly upon economic interests and legal rights (Sandel [1982] [1996]). It remains to be seen to what extent Sandel would commit himself to global public issues such as world peace, nuclear weapons, nuclear power, environmental problems, and so on.[11]

M. Walzer, on the other hand, regards himself as a particularist and emphasizes that the goods in several spheres of society should be distributed according to their social meaning in each community. Furthermore, goods such as money and political power should not dominate the distribution of goods in other areas. According to Walzer's ideas of "complex equality," inequalities in the various spheres of society must not invade one another (Walzer [1983]). Walzer argues further with regard to *the Divided Self*. The Self divides itself in terms of its social roles as a citizen, worker, teacher, parent, etc., defines its identity in terms of its family, nation, religion, and gender, and further divides itself among its ideals, principles, and values as a subject to internal reflection and to any criticism. According to Walzer, it is these *Divided Selves* that are fit for a differentiated and pluralist society (Walzer [1994] Chapter 5).

---

11 Recently, Sandel made his speech several times not only in Japan but also in Korea and China. However, he seems not to have committed himself to such serious problems as war and peace, nuclear weapons, nuclear energy, and so on.

Walzer criticizes, however, any universalistic and cosmopolitan ideas, because they deny the particularities of communities and nations. Instead, he introduces the dual moral of *Thick* and *Thin*. *Thick morals* are valid in the familiar cultural world or communities, while *thin morals* are valid in unfamiliar cultural worlds or communities. Walzer assumes that such an idea makes it possible to create international solidarities against political oppression etc. without falling into abstract cosmopolitanism (Walzer [1994] Chapter 1, 4). In this regard, he supports a *thin idea of global civil society* (Walzer [1995]), which I will take up in the fourth chapter. However, he rejects any cosmopolitanism and, accordingly, the idea of a Cosmopolitan Self. Indeed, on this point, our concept of *glocal* public philosophy as also stressing the *dimension of the Cosmopolitan Self* differs from Walzer's communitarianism.

b) MacIntyre and Bellah

While these two communitarians' thoughts show doubtlessly American traits, A. MacIntyre's social thought rests upon the *Aristotelian or Thomistic tradition*, which attaches much importance to *civic virtue and common good*. Moreover, MacIntyre emphasizes the "narrative character" of human identity and the "tradition-laden" character of rationality. It is important for Macintyre that each person, seeking the virtuous life, establishes an individual identity by telling a narrative about himself or herself in his or her own public world, which is culturally as well as historically characterized (MacIntyre [1981] [1988]).

In my view, although he favors the Aristotelian and Thomistic tradition too much, MacIntyre's idea of *narrative Self* in one's own cultural tradition can be integrated into our concept of *glocal* public philosophy.

R. Bellah, on the other hand, could be regarded as an American public philosopher with a cosmopolitan mind. To be sure, his books *Habits of Hearts* [1985] and *The Good Society* [1991] both treat specific American problems. Criticizing the egoistic individualism and utilitarianism dominant in the US, Bellah advocates the reconstruction of the public mind, public philosophy, and even public church. In this sense, he is categorized among American communitarians, but he had studied Japanese modern social thought and associated with many Japanese public intellectuals; including Maruyama Masao, as will be discussed in Chapter 3 (Bellah [2003]). Bellah's concern in later life was seeking a global civil religion based upon human rights, against not only a neo-liberal economy but also nationalism (Bellah [2014]). In this respect, it should be pointed out that Bellah criticized Walzer, who denies any kind of cosmopolitanism. It is a pity that he passed away without developing this new orientation.

From the viewpoint of *glocal* philosophy, these communitarian ideas deserve attention and praise because they offer an *ontological starting point for thinking about the Self and the Public World,* as well as an *ethical starting point for thinking about social (common) goods and civic virtue*. The ontological as well as ethical starting points offered by the so-called communitarians, however, seem to be insufficient, because these viewpoints are limited to the Anglo-American World and lack thoughts on the trans-national public world and people outside the US, although the last work of Bellah [2014] seems to break through this limit. Therefore, we have to modify these scholars' thoughts in light of *glocal* public philosophy.

2.2.5 Hannah Arendt and Jürgen Habermas – Public Sphere and Communicative Action

Distinct from these trends, the abovementioned two orthodox German philosophers, Hannah Arendt and Jürgen Habermas, created alternative starting points for public philosophy.

a) Arendt

As stated above, Arendt in *The Human Condition* [1958] formulated the notion of publicness or the public realm as the "open space of appearance and common world for us." According to her, it is nothing but the action distinguished from labor and work that makes the open space of appearance and the common world. In such public actions, each human being communicates with one another by means of language and engages in self-realization. Such public actions played a very important role in the Greek polis yet disappeared in modern times, because labor and private property became cardinal constituents in the political world. Criticizing this modern tendency, Arendt aimed to rehabilitate the public actions of citizens and to activate the *Political* in distinction from the *Social*, which implies the conformity of the world (Arendt [1958] pp. 38-49). On the basis of this idea, Arendt tackled lots of public issues with which she was confronted, such as totalitarianism, diaspora, Eichmann's trial, violence, revolution, etc., and published many articles and books.[12]

I highly estimate Arendt's public philosophy, especially because it has laid a *quasi-ontological foundation for publicness or the public realm* in terms of action, speech, communication, and the common world. Indeed, it offers us a viewpoint to understand and discuss the *Public World* together with the concept of *Self and Others*. Nevertheless, I do not share her exclusion of the "Social" from the public world, and I therefore differ from her in that she did not regard economic-social problems as public issues and consequently disregarded social policy. On the contrary, in my view, economic-social problems are important elements of public issues, and social economic policy must become an important element of public philosophy.

[12] For an excellent overview of Arendt's political works, see Canovan [1994].

b) Habermas

Habermas' public philosophy offers us a different viewpoint from Arendt's. As stated above, Habermas came from the Critical Theory school of Horkheimer and Adorno, which adopted a Marxian critique of capitalistic society, while Arendt was influenced by philosophical ontology as a former student of Heidegger and criticized Marx harshly. Taking over the positive legacy of Critical Theory, Habermas developed his normative theory, which attaches great importance to the formation of consensus based upon the communicative actions of citizens in the public space (Habermas [1981]). According to him, one needs a discourse ethics as "duty ethics" (deontology) in order to perform communicative actions distinguished from any strategic actions. His discourse ethics demands "the truth of proposition, the normative rightness and the subjective sincereness of each participant" (Habermas [1991]).

Therefore, it could be said that Habermas' concept of communicative action is almost synonymous with consensus-oriented public discussion. As a matter of fact, Habermas has no sympathy with communitarians in the US, stressing the priority of the right to the good in the public spheres (like Rawls). On the other hand, he emphasizes the significance of "solidarity," which is not synonymous with justice, to realize democracy and to reach the consensus in the public sphere. His last political dream is to establish the *European Constitution* by the democratic consensus of the European people (Habermas [2011]).

Although I appreciate this conception and intention on the part of Habermas, I have to say that his public philosophy is *too idealistic* as well as *too Eurocentric* for people living outside Europe to realize. Even for European citizens, it is not so easy to meet the demands of discourse ethics, because it overestimates the "communicative reason in the form of discourse." Though Habermas began to appreciate the altruistic power of religion, especially of Christianity, to perform discourse ethics since the 2000s, it is extremely difficult to perform discourse ethics outside Europe. In addition, Habermas has been negative in introducing the ontological concept of Self and World from his viewpoint of "post-metaphysical thinking." In my view, such post-metaphysical thinking is less flexible than dogmatic when taking the diversity of the world's cultures into consideration. That is why I differ from Habermas in terms of our public philosophy, although I attach much importance to his idea of *public sphere and civil society*, as I will take up in Chapter 4.

2.2.6 Transition to Our Idea of Glocal Public Philosophy in View of Northeast Asian Countries

As I said in the first note of the previous chapter, there has been an independent development of public philosophy in Japanese academia since the end of the 20th century. The academia in China and South Korea, too, has gradually become familiar with the new academic concept of public philosophy. Fortunately, the above-discussed public philosophies in Western countries have already been imported in these Northeast Asian countries. Indeed, it is a necessary condition for public philosophers in Northeast Asian countries to understand the traits of representative public philosophies in Western countries so as to develop public philosophy in Northeast Asia. On the other hand, though, the modern histories of Japan, China and Korea differ from one another quite markedly.

In my view, even among the public philosophies in Western countries, each bears its own historical and cultural background or context, as was seen in Lippmann, Dewey, Rawls, the communitarians, Arendt, and Habermas. In this sense, it might be said that these intellectuals or philosophers committed themselves from *their own particular viewpoints*. However, apart from Walzer (who declares his position as a particularist), it can be said that many of them have *non-particularistic dimensions of ideas concerning Self, social (common) goods, and civic virtue*. In other words, they also have more or less transversal or cross-cultural elements, open to discussion for people all over the world.

With this consideration, I will elaborate my idea of *glocal* public philosophy.

2.3 Normative and Descriptive Understanding of Self, Others, and Public World as *Glocal Ontology*

I would like to begin by repeating one passage from the last part of the previous chapter:

> *Glocal public philosophy can be defined as a trans-national public philosophy, which deals with global issues not from nowhere but from somewhere to be locally characterized. What is important is the correlation between the globality of public issues and the historically, as well as culturally, characterized localities in which each human being lives …* To reinforce this program, however, a *new theory of Self, Others, and Public World* is needed … It is important for a *glocal* public philosophy to develop an ontological foundation in a comprehensive way in to avoid falling into any ethnocentrism or irresponsible rootless universalism.

Based upon this idea, I introduced the concept of the *Multidimensional Self* that includes both the *Cosmopolitan Self* and the *locally situated Particular Self*. This *Multidimensional Self* understands itself, without losing its cosmopolitan dimension of the Self, in a multidimensional way; moreover, it also understands *Others* who live in various cultural and historical contexts, as well as the *Public World* where each individual lives in a multidimensional way. On this point, the ontology of the *Multidimensional Self* both agrees and disagrees with the above-described communitarian idea of the Self.

Now, I will develop this ontology in a more normative way so that the *glocal* public philosophy can offer more practical traits. For this purpose, I will make use of the hermeneutic insight stated above.

As Heidegger described in *Sein und Zeit*, I start from the viewpoint that each human being lives under his or her contingent conditions in the world. Concretely saying, each individual cannot choose the body with which he or she is born. Each also cannot choose the cultural and historical circumstances into which he or she is born. In this regard, it seems that the human being is not free but determined by nature. This fact is, however, only half a truth. In contrast to other animals, the human being is capable of making his or her living as he or she wants. The human being is also capable of making the given world changeable into a better one. In this respect, human beings can become free from fates and misfortunes, and I call such a creative dimension of the human being the *Becoming Self*.

This *Becoming Self* in our sense is naturally distinct from Heidegger's *Dasein*, because the *Becoming Self* pays positive attention and attaches much importance to the *Public World* in which he or she lives. Although Heidegger in *Sein und Zeit* referred to *Mitsein* (being with others) and *Sorge* (care), he meant by that an unauthentic way of living (Heidegger [1927] § 25-27, § 39-44). Moreover, as was pointed out above, his concept of the public sphere was conceived in a totally negative way. In other words, there is no ethical way to solve the public issues in his ontology. He has not only been interested in communication with *Others who live in different cultural and historical circumstances* but also with *public values* such as peace, justice, human rights, and so on.

In this respect, *glocal* public philosophy parts from Heidegger and comes nearer to Arendt's public philosophy. As I said already, however, Arendt limited her scope to political affairs and showed little interest in economic-social problems or the notion of civil society, while *glocal* public philosophy tries always to deal not only with political affairs but also with economic-social problems in civil society (which I will treat in Chapter 4).

In view of the history of philosophy, one might think that this idea of *Becoming Self* is reminiscent of Hegel's *Phenomenology of Minds* (Hegel [1952/1807]). However, there is a distinction between them. Namely, the *Becoming Self* in *glocal* public philosophy always makes efforts to change its mind for the better and consequently always understands itself as a *finite being* who can never reach the "Absolute Knowledge" as Hegel assumed (ibid. VIII pp. 549 564). In this regard, the *Becoming Self* must be also called the *Dialogical and Responsible Self*, who is always ready for dialog with others and even *metanoia* (change in one's way of living, resulting from penitence of spiritual conversion), to which the Japanese philosopher Tanabe Hajime attached much importance. I will treat his original ontology in Chapter 3.

As for the *Public World* in which each human being lives, it differs from the concept of the "Life World" in phenomenological philosophy and sociology in several points.[13] First, it is conceived as the world of *various public values* such as peace, justice, human rights, environmental preservation, etc. Second, it includes *public bads or evils*, such as war, violence, injustice, violation of human rights, environmental destruction, and even natural disaster. On this point, we can still much learn from the heritage of the Critical Theory stated above. At any rate, the *Public World* contains both *public values* to be realized and *public bads or evils* to be eliminated. It is of great importance for the *glocal* public philosophy that *each Self* tries to address such public values and bads or evils from each situation in cooperation with *Others*. Thus, the ontology of Self, Others, and Public World in *glocal* public philosophy requires the *normative understanding* of Self, Others, and Public World.

The *glocal* public philosophy cannot, however, remain only on the normative level. It requires *descriptive-analytical understanding, especially of the Public World,* in order to avoid falling into idealism. In my view, public philosophers such as Dewey, Rawls, the communitarians, and even Habermas seem to lack the analytical description of the public world as comprising social realities. As a matter of fact, there has been a communication gap between public philosophy and the social sciences, which can be regarded as a relic of the period of specialization. However, such a gap must be overcome in the *period of post-specialization*, which means that the relationship between the social sciences and philosophy, including ethics, must become closer again. It is in this period that *glocal* public philosophy finds its place.

From this perspective, the role of various social sciences including political science, economics, sociology, ecology, and history that try to analyze, describe, and understand social realities must be seen as very important. In my view, not only Max Weber's *sociology of understanding based upon Ideal-Types* (Weber [1968/1904]) but also Karl Popper's idea of *problem-solving piecemeal social engineering according to various situations* (which, as mentioned above, tries to combine social analysis with social policy in its own ethical viewpoint of open society and negative utilitarianism) can play a very important role for the descriptive understanding of the public world (Popper [1957], [1984]). In sum, *glocal public philosophy requires both normative and descriptive understanding of Public World, Self, and Others*, which I would like to call *Glocal Ontology*.

[13] Phenomenological sociology represented by Alfred Schütz [1974] seems to make no distinction between the *social world* in general and the *public world* characterized by public values.

2.4 A Three-dimensional Method of Learning and Ethics for *Glocal* Public Philosophy

Based upon the statement above, I would like to propose the *integration of a three-dimensional method of learning* in the sense of the process of gaining knowledge through studying (see *Cobuild Advanced Learner's English Dictionary, New Digital Edition*) and *of ethics* in the broad sense to construct *glocal* public philosophy in the *period of post-specialization*.

2.4.1 Integration of a Three-dimensional Method of Learning in the Period of Post-specialization

I begin to discuss the possible ways of integrating the following three methods of leaning.

a) *Empirical research on social realities in the past and present.* It does not matter whether its method is based on the ideal-type in Weber's sense, the problem-solving method of Critical Rationalism in Popper's sense, the Critical Theory in Horkheimer's sense, or the critical insight about mass media that Lippmann once displayed, so far as it relates to the philosophical question *what must we know?*
b) *Normative theory of present and future societies.* This relates to the question *what should we think, judge, and do?* To this question, we have to develop critically the heritages of the pubic philosophers described above, such as Dewey, Rawls, Sen, Nussbaum, the communitarians, and Habermas, further from the *glocal* point of view.
c) *The socio-political issue on the feasibility of norms for the future.* This relates to the question *what can we perform?* To this question, Popper's ideas of piecemeal social engineering described above can offer a helpful example, but we have to adopt a more holistic form of social policy, such as system theory based on complex studies.

What is important here is to integrate this tripartite method of learning "through interdisciplinary collaboration" in which each philosopher, social scientist, technologist, and even natural scientist takes part in his or her own way. As a matter of fact, there are numerous *glocal* public issues in the world such as war and peace, nuclear weapons, nuclear energy, global warming, human rights, justice, poverty, wellbeing, etc., that require public discussions and interdisciplinary collaborations. This fact then leads us to the *method of public ethics for the glocal philosophy*.

2.4.2 Integration of a Three-dimensional Ethics for the Trans-national Public Ethics

In the previous chapter, I discussed *transnational public ethics* from several viewpoints. Based on this conception, I would like to introduce a *three-dimensional trans-national ethics* that consists of *positive and negative values, duty ethics, and virtue ethics,* which must be integrated into the *glocal* public philosophy.

a) Ethics of Positive Public Values and Negative Values

As noted in the previous chapter, the classical founders of the ethics of public or common goods were Thomas Aquinas[14] and Friedrich Schleiermacher [2002/1812-17]. In the unstable age of globalization today, the ethics of public or common good must include the public bad or evil, which I would like to call the public bad or evil *negative values*, while I call the public or common good *positive public values*. Therefore, I formulate this dimension of ethics as that of positive public values and negative values.

It is a very important task to develop this kind of ethics on the trans-national level. We can regard world peace, human rights, world cultural or natural heritage, world health, human securities, etc., as trans-national positive values. On the other hand, we can regard wars, terrorism, political oppression, starvation, contagious disease, environmental destruction, etc., as trans-national negative values. As for the concept of "social capital" in the sense of the value of network (Putnam [1993]), we have to judge whether it is a positive or negative value according to each case. Generally speaking, the social capital that contributes to trans-national positive value mentioned above can be seen as a positive value, too, while the social capital of the Mafia, terrorists, etc., can be seen as negative values.

In this regard, I make use of a remarkable report by the United Nations Development Programme, as was mentioned in the previous chapter. According to this report, trans-national public values consist of "natural global commons," such as the ozone layer, atmosphere, and climate, "human-made global commons," such as norms and principles accepted worldwide (e.g., universal human rights), scientific knowledge, the internet, etc., and "global policy outcomes," including peace, health, and stable financial markets.

Trans-national negative values include the depletion of the ozone layer and increased levels of radiation, the risk of global warming, violation of human rights, injustice, lack of equal rights, exclusion and inequality of access in regard to information, wars and conflict, epidemics, and financial crises, among others.[15] In addition, weapons of massive destruction must be regarded as trans-national negative values. As regards nuclear power plants that caused public evils in Fukushima

---

14 On the contemporary relevance of the common good theory of Aquinas, see Keys [2008].

15 See Kaul et al. [1999].

recently, opinions would be divided on whether they constitute a positive or negative value. I will discuss this matter intensively in Chapter 5.

What I would like to add to these elements is the *trans-national public memory*. The memory of negative values means the memory of wars, starvation, political oppression, the arrogance of cultural imperialism, environmental destruction, barbarous acts of modern sovereign states, oppression of one people by other people, religious intolerance, etc. The memory of positive values includes the memory of peace, wellbeing of peoples, emancipation of peoples from oppression, the building of a constitutional state, etc. These memories must be shared and discussed on the trans-national level.

In order to formulate this mode of ethics, we need the *trans-national civil society and global governance,* which means cooperation between civil society organizations such as INGO and United Nations organizations such as UNESCO, UNICEF, ILO, WHO, etc. I will detail the reformulation of civil society in Chapter 4.

b) Duty-based Ethics (deontology)

To realize the trans-national positive values and to diminish negative values, it would be necessary to devise a *duty-based ethics concerning trans-national public rules and orders*; not only on the part of institutions or organizations but also with respect to the power of peoples.

In *Perpetual Peace*, published in 1795, Kant advanced his own ideas of the "Preliminary Articles and three Definitive Articles" (Kant [1970/1795] pp.93-108). I do not enter into details here and, instead, note that he emphasized a league of free states as a basis of the law of nations, and universal hospitality as a basis of the law of world citizenship. To establish such a world citizenship was regarded not as a duty of each individual but as the task of peaceful governments.

Nowadays, the duty-based ethics for trans-national values must be pursued not only by governments but by trans-national civil society and global government. Cooperation between liberal societies and illiberal but decent hierarchical societies, as Rawls conceived in his last work *The Law of Peoples* (Rawls [1999] Part II pp. 59-88), is insufficient. To perform this task, however, cooperation between peaceful governments and trans-national civil societies is indispensable. Therefore, the narrow concept of "public reason" conceived by Rawls (ibid., pp. 164-175) must be broadened into *trans-national civil society* cooperating intensively for more peaceful and just societies.

c) Virtue Ethics

Although duty is an important component of ethics, it tends to evoke a limited and narrow impression among the people. *Glocal* public ethics that requires the normative orientation of the Self would probably only attain greater vitality through virtue ethics, which is centered on spontaneous or responsive human behavior and the happiness of human beings. Indeed, classic philosophy in both Europe and Japan developed on the basis of virtue.

As I cited in the previous chapter, it was Spinoza who emphasized the role of virtue ethics for peace. He wrote that "peace is not the absence of war; it is a virtue, a state of mind, a disposition of benevolence, confidence, justice." He conceived the best state (commonwealth) as one in which the people live in harmony. Such a state is established by a free people, who are led more by hope than by fear (Spinoza [1958]).

What is important, especially for virtue ethics, is happiness and benevolence.[16]

According to Aristotle, the founder of virtue ethics in Western philosophy, nothing but happiness is the goal of human social behavior. Happiness lies in an active reality of the soul in accord with virtue (*arête*) (Aristotle [2000]). In the East Asian classical ethics of Confucianism, goodness, justice, etiquette, wisdom, and honesty are regarded as fundamental virtues. These virtues also provide the basis of the notion of *Keiseisaimin* (経世済民) (social policy for relieving the suffering of the people), which has been widespread in Japan since the *Edo era*.

Trans-national virtue ethics must break the national boundary to which Aristotle and the Confucians were limited and seek *Co-happiness* among peoples all over the world. I would like to treat this theme in the last chapter of this book.

By way of concluding remarks in this chapter, I would like to stress that *these three-dimensional trans-national ethics must be combined with the ontological basis of* the *Multidimensional and Becoming Self, who tackles public issues from each glocal situation of the public world in cooperation with Others*. Thus, it is imperative for the *glocal* public philosophy to integrate three-dimensional Ethics; three-dimensional Ontology of Self, Others, and Public World; and three-dimensional Methodology of Learning for the realization of more peaceful and just societies.

16 For this theme, see Spaemann [1989].

3 Rethinking the Legacy of Public Philosophies in Modern Japan

In this chapter, I would like to reconsider the legacy of public philosophies from the latter half of the 1920s to the 1990s in Japan. This reconsideration is all the more important because this period featured dramatic changes within the Japanese public sphere.

To pursue this theme, I will first take up three philosophers from the time period in question: Tanabe, Watsuji, and Miki, who derived, more or less, from the tradition of the so-called Kyoto School and developed their own ideas of social philosophy or ethics from the latter half of the 1920s to the 1940s. I will add to them the failure of the attempt to overcome European modernity, as advanced by some scholars in the Kyoto School at that time.

After this, I will take up two philosophers, Nanbara and Maruyama, who developed their own ideas against the background of post-WWII Japan. Lastly, I will address the legacy of other public philosophies in post-WWII Japan.

3.1 Critical Reappraisal of the Heritage of the Kyoto School

The three philosophers that I treat in this part can be regarded as orthodox philosophers who related, more or less, to the thinking of Nishida Kitarō (1870-1945): the founder of what has been called *the Kyoto School of Philosophy*. Acquiring many Western philosophies in his own way and incorporating Buddhism ideas, Nishida developed a very original philosophy. His cardinal ideas were *Self-awareness* (自覚), *Absolute Nothingness* (絶対無), and *Locus* (場 *Ba* in Japanese), which characterizes the dynamic relation of Self-becoming to World-formation (Nishida [1993/1945]). Partly influenced by Nishida's philosophy, the following three philosophers criticized or abandoned the highly abstract traits of Nishida's ideas and, instead, developed their own social philosophy or ethics that we could call public philosophies. In spite of the limits of the days in which they lived, I think the *legacy of their own public philosophy must be reconsidered from the viewpoint of glocal* public philosophy.[1]

[1] For a recent introduction to the Kyoto School in which Nishida, Tanabe, Watsuji, and Others are expounded, see Carter [2013].

3.1.1 From Logic of Species to Metanoetics: In the Case of Tanabe Hajime (田辺元 1885-1962)

I begin with Tanabe Hajime, who was a great philosopher of the Kyoto School.

After being invited to Kyoto University by Nishida in 1919 and studying at Marburg University in Germany from 1922 to 1924, Tanabe began to develop his own philosophy under the influence of German idealism; especially Kant and Hegel. Though Tanabe respected Nishida, who began to discuss the significance of the historical world in the 1930s, he could not be satisfied with Nishida's *Logic of Locus* (*Ba*).[2]

I summarize his main thought before, during, and after the Second World War.

From 1934 to 1935, Tanabe published *The Logic of Social Being* and advanced his social philosophy. He also published another two books in the following two years to complement the previous book. According to Tanabe, the idea of interaction and dialog between Self and Others developed by Nishida is not sufficient to grasp socio-historical realities, because it lacks "mediation" between Self and Others. Therefore, in order to express this mediation, the *logic of species* （種） must be introduced and developed. The Self as individual is absolutely mediated by species, which forms the concrete socio-historical world. The subjectivism of modern philosophy ignores this aspect. Even Heidegger's *Being and Time (Sein und Zeit)*, which intends to overcome subjectivism, is deficient, because the time and historicity of the individual must be understood in connection with the *historically mediated concrete Self* as a social being (Tanabe [2010/1934-37] pp. 11-186).

In this regard, Tanabe highly appreciated Hegel's criticism of Kant in his *Philosophy of Right (Philosophie des Rechts)*. As is widely known, Hegel criticized Kant's abstract idea of morality because it cannot comprehend social and ethical institutions; consequently, Hegel put forward the idea of *Sittlichkeit*, which consists of the family, bourgeois society, and the state (Hegel [1970/1821]). Tanabe agrees with this idea and regards the state as the top ethical institution (Tanabe ibid. pp. 350-352, p. 440). In addition, Tanabe emphasizes that the *self-consciousness of an institutionally mediated Self* must be based upon religious consciousness. For Tanabe, Self-affirmation must be realized by means of *Self-negation* as emancipation from egoism and selfishness. Thus, in Tanabe's *Logic of Species*, Self is characterized not only as social-ethical but also *religious*. Likewise, the social world is characterized as not only historical and ethical but also *religious* (ibid. p. 406).

It must be pointed out, however, that Tanabe did not conceive of the world state, although he admitted its significance as a genus that is higher than the state (ibid. pp. 132-133). Indeed, it was during the middle of the 1930s that Tanabe's social philosophy was advanced. Japan invaded China in those days and withdrew

2 For Tanabe's philosophy in general, see Carter [2013] pp. 61-89 and Ozaki [2001].

from the *League of Nations* after being subject to its condemnation. Tanabe's combination of state and religion posed a danger in that it affirmed the totalitarian ideology of the Japanese imperial state. Accordingly, Nanbara Shigeru, whom I will take up later in this chapter, justly criticized him in 1942 during the war period (Nanbara [2014/1942] pp. 314-327).

After the Second World War, Tanabe restarted his philosophical thinking, introducing new ideas and critically modifying his former ideas. The crucial new idea is characterized by *Philosophy of Metanoetics* (懺悔道の哲学), which was published in 1946 (Tanabe [2010/1946], [1990/1946]). Regretting his incompetence with regard to the totalitarian system of prewar Japan, he said the following in the Preface:

> The only thing for me to do in the situation was to resign myself honestly to my weakness, to examine my own inner self with humility, and to explore the depth of my powerless and lack of freedom. Would not this mean a new task to take the place of the philosophical task that had previously engaged me?. … The decision was reached. … through metanoia, or the way of *zange*, and led *to a philosophy that is not a philosophy*: philosophy seen as self-realization of *metanoetic consciousness*.

(Tanabe [2010] pp. 36-37, [1990] Preface).

Thus, starting from his own experience, Tanabe began to develop a new practical thinking named matanoetics. It was *Shinran*'s (1173-1262親鸞) thought of *Other-power* (他力) that Tanabe relied on for his new start. Shinran was a very famous founder of *Shin-Buddhism* (浄土真宗) and preached salvation by the *Other-power of Amida* (阿弥陀). According to Tanabe, *Other-power* brings about a conversion in one's own Self and heads an individual in a new direction. *Zange* means repentance for the wrongs one's own Self has done, with the accompanying torment of knowing that there is no way to expiate one's sins. It also signifies shame over powerlessness and inability. However, *Zange* also represents an experience of *Other-power* acting in and through *Zange* to urge the Self to a new advance in philosophy. It could be said that it is a kind of conversion-and-resurrection of the Self (Tanabe [2010/1947], [1990/1947] Chap. 1).

Indeed, this new way of thinking based on his own experience shows Tanabe's radical turn. It would be wrong, however, to think that Tanabe completely changed his former thought, because he still did not abandon his *Logic of Species* (although he modified it to some extent) (ibid. Chap. 8). The Self who relies on *Other-power* is conceived as being absolutely mediated by social and ethical institutions. In this regard, Tanabe's idea of Self still stands in the Hegelian tradition. In my view, one crucial difference between *Logic of Species* and *Philosophy of Metanoetics* lies in the fact that Tanabe pays much importance to the problem of evil in the latter. As a matter of fact, he appreciated Schelling's thought on freedom and evil much more in the latter than in the former. He intended, moreover, to overcome the excessively theoretical tendency of Schelling via the *practice of Zange* (ibid. Chap. 4).

Japanese people should, Tanabe says, convert themselves spiritually. Changing his former social philosophy in this way, Tanabe never abandoned his commitment to political and social issues after WWII, and he was therefore obliged to promote solidarity with other peoples. In my view, this attitude made him a genuine public philosopher, though he did not know the name of public philosophy. As for historical consciousness, Tanabe rejected the view of the progress of history and emphasized the role of the present in which the Self recollects the past and combines it with the future. The historical world should be always innovated by the *menatoetic consciousness of the Self* in this way (ibid. Chap. 3). For Tanabe, the public world consists of not only social and historical elements but also a religious element for which each Self takes responsibility.

More concretely, Tanabe advocated a farewell to the totalitarian Japanese state in the prewar time based upon metanoetic consciousness of each Japanese person, and he stressed "fraternity or solidarity" that combines freedom with equality. Tanabe rejected the liberal or egalitarian Self that has no idea of metanoetic consciousness. Moreover, he emphasized the *Great Compassion* (大悲), a very important public value of Buddhism, to strengthen the feeling of solidarity with other suffering peoples all over the world (ibid. See the last parts of chap 8 and also [1975]). Evidently, Tanabe's former logic of species shifted its emphasis from the nation state to the international world. Differing from democrats such as Maruyama Masao (whom I will discuss later in this chapter), however, Tanabe did not attach so much importance to democracy, because he thought that democracy without metanoetic consciousness and the feeling of compassion would be empty. He also mentioned the *danger of nuclear energy in the public world* as a product of modern technology (Tanabe [1975/1950]). This is not seen in Nanbara and Maruyama's progressivist thoughts, to be described below in 3.2.

Thus, Tanabe's public philosophy after WWII can be re-appreciated in terms of the dynamic relationship between the *Becoming Self* and *Public World*. Indeed, it was a very deep, passionate, and moving public philosophy. Nevertheless, it must be pointed out that there remains a desideratum for his thought of *other selves* and the *public world*. To be sure, he stressed solidarity with not only Japanese people but also other peoples all over the people. Still, he hardly referred to the peoples in East Asian countries that Japan had colonized in the prewar time. The modern histories of other East Asian countries are quite different from that of Japan. This desideratum makes us suspect that Tanabe ignored these other Asian peoples and their histories.

Moreover, Tanabe's *Logic of Species* lacks the dimension of *civil society* in the positive sense. Although he was familiar with Hegelian ides of civil society,

Tanabe did not pay so much attention to the public role of civil society; especially in comparison with the attention that Hegel devoted to the Corporation, etc. It seems never to have occurred to Tanabe to conceive the *trans-national civil society* in distinction from the state. The idea of the historical and religious world in *Logic of Species* has a weakness in this respect.

If we were to take over the legacy of Tanabe's deeply religious public philosophy, we would thus have to make up for these desiderata.

3.1.2 From Hermeneutical Relational Ethics via Ethnocentric Nationalism to Cultural Conservatism: In the Case of Watsuji Tetsuro (和辻哲郎 1889-1960)

Now, I would like to treat the works of Watsuji, who has been regarded as a very famous ethicist and cultural philosopher. His works range over various topics in the arts, religions, cultures, and history of thought both in the East and the West. However, the core of his achievements is undoubtedly the ethical thought that was developed from the 1930s to the 1940s after his time studying in Germany from 1927-1928.[3]

In his very popular book titled *Ethics as the Science of the Human Being*, published in 1934 and dedicated to Nishida Kitaro, Watsiji claims that ethics must be founded on a solid anthropological basis, which modern individualistic ethics has failed to consider. Kantian ethics, for example, rests upon an overly individualistic and abstract concept of man and thus fails to take the whole reality of the human being into consideration. Even the attempt to transform Kantian ethics into social democratic ethics by Hermann Cohen (1842-1918), whose name was fairly well known among intellectuals at that time, is bound by a similarly abstract concept. According to Watsuji, the failure of Kantian ethics in general is due to its individualistic or formalistic view of human beings and society (Watshuji [2007/1934] Chap. 7-8, pp. 69-102)

What Watsuji advocates instead is a *relational ethics* grounded on the new concept of the human being. The character *Ningen* (人間), which means human being in Japanese, implies that the human being does not exist alone but "between human being and human being." In this sense, the human being is by nature a social being, and ethics cannot exist except as social ethics. The problem of what should be and what one should do therefore always has to be discussed in the context of relation (ibid. Chap. 1-2). Based upon this view of the human being, Watstuji declares his method of ethics as "hermeneutical." According to him, both Heidegger's hermeneutical phenomenology adopted for his original work *Being and Time* (*Sein und Zeit*) and Dilthey's hermeneutical concepts such as lived experiences,

[3] For Watsuji's philosophy in general, see Carter [2013] 125-152. For a critical study on Watsuji, see Bellah [2003] pp. 114-139.

expression, and understanding are insufficient to understand the *relational ethical being* (ibid. Chap. 15, pp. 214-233).

To be sure, it was a great endeavor that Heidegger attempted, employing hermeneutical phenomenology to understand the human being in the world from the perspective of its temporality and historicity. His attempt lacks, however, consideration of the *ethical* relationship of human beings, although he introduced the concept of *Mitsein* (*being together*), which Watsuji regards as a variation of the solipsistic way of thinking. In this regard, Watsuji favored Dilthey's hermeneutical idea of *Leben (life)* and *Ausdruck (expression)* over Heidegger's *Mitsein,* because the former implies a positive relationship between human beings. Still, Dilthey's hermeneutical idea of life remains too abstract to grasp the *ethical* relationship between human beings. The hermeneutical method must be applied to ethics in order to understand the concrete everyday ethical life of human beings. In this regard, the *Hermeneutical Self* must be understood as the *Ethical Self*, and hermeneutics must become *hermeneutical relational Ethics* (ibid. Chap 16.pp. 233-258).

Following this idea of hermeneutical relational ethics, Watshuji developed his more comprehensive thought in his major work entitled *Ethics* (倫理学 *Rinrigaku*), which was published from 1937 to 1949 (Watshiji [2004/1936-49], [1996]). In the introduction to this thick book, Watsuiji emphasizes the notion of *Yononaka* (世の中) or *Seken* (世間) in Japanese, which could be translated as the public world in English. The public world in the sense of Yononaka or Seken is closely connected with *Ningen* (人間 human being) and therefore must not be confused with the modern concept of bourgeois society (in German, *Gesellschaft*). As a matter of fact, each human being always lives in the public world as *an ethical, historical, and climatic world*.

Based upon this fundamental thought, Watsuji systematically deals with the ethical problems of private and public existence, the family, relatives, local communities, economical systems, cultural community, and nation, which taken together form a hierarchical value. As for the *problem of private and public*, Watsuji regards the relational element of the human being as a *public* existence and the individual element of the human being as a *private* existence, which therefore means a "deficiency of public being" (Watshuji [2004/1936-49] Chap. 2, section 1, [1996] Chap. 8). In his view, a private being can be said, in essence, to be public. The public existence and world have "hierarchical dimensions" ranging from the family to the nation, as shown above. The family has a private character in relation to local community, and the local community has a private character in relation to nation. Watsuji did not think, however, at least in the prewar period, that the nation has a private character in relation to humankind, and he instead only referred to the international world in which the media plays both a positive and negative role (ibid. Chap. 3, section 7).

Now, I have to say that Watsuji's ethics reveals its nationalistic traits in the last respect noted above. Watsuji insists that cultures are deeply rooted in national particularities or peculiarities and that, therefore, cosmopolitanism without regard to them is not only illusionary but also undesirable. This kind of cultural nationalism is reminiscent of Herder, who, around the late 18th century, was opposed to Kantian universalism for its cultural-national theory. As a matter of fact, Watsuji in his younger days introduced Herder in Japan and published in 1935, at the time between *Ethics as the Science of the Human Being* and *Ethics (Rinrigaku)*, a very famous book on the comparative study of culture entitled *Fudo,* which has been translated into several languages (Watsuji [1979/1935], [1988/1935]).[4]

Fudo means, as it were, "The way of life conditioned by the climate." Watsuji classifies three types of *Fudo* in this book. First is the *type of monsoon climate* to which India, China, Japan, and other countries in Southeast Asia belong, and which forms receptive resigned spirits. Second is the *type of desert zone* represented by African, Muslim, and Judean culture, characterized by a resistant and fighting spirit. Third is the *type of meadow* represented by Greek and European cultures, characterized by rational spirit and conquest of nature (ibid. Chap. 2).

Although this theory of *Fudo* features multi-cultural traits, it could be wrong to believe that Watsuji is a cultural relativist, for his cultural theory was closely combined with his nationalism. In an article written during the wartime, Watsuji stressed that Anglo-American civilization is characterized by F. Bacon's, as well as Hobbes', individualism (Watsuji [1944]). According to him, American history is nothing but an invasion into the land of aboriginal people such as Indian people. Likewise, the *Declaration of Independence* was merely written for Anglo-American people and rests upon the total disregard of black people and slavery. It is the same exclusive mentality that Commodore Perry brought to Japan in 1853, resulting in the suppression of Japan. Therefore, the war between the US and Japan should be regarded as a clash between American individualistic-egoistic-utilitarian civilization and Japanese relational-ethical culture, which can emancipate other Asian people from the dependency of Anglo-American imperialism. Thus, Watsuji became one of the representative ethnocentric nationalists during the wartime.

In post-WWII Japan, however, Watsuji modified this thought and adopted a rather moderate cultural conservatism. He recognized the constitutional monarchy and the representative democracy, as well as trans-national organizations such as the UN. He also criticized the closed nationalism in Japan, as expressed in his book on the period of national isolation in the Edo era (Watsuji [1982/1950]).

What is the legacy of Watsuji? In my view, his positive legacy is his thinking about the *climatic and cultural particularities of the public world*, which reminds us of Montesquieu and Herder. As French anthropogeographer and thinker Au-

[4] For Watsuji's appraisal of Herder, see Watsuji [1979/1988/1935] Chap 5.

gustin Berque pointed out,[5] it may be Watsuji's cultural way of thinking about the public world that can cope with the homogenous global ideology today. In this sense, Watsuji can be regarded as an original public philosopher from whom we can learn much. This positive legacy, however, has to dispose of his negative legacies such as ethnocentrism and, instead, add the dimension of *trans-national public values and civil society*. In short, Watsuji's positive legacy should not be rehabilitated as a *national public philosophy* but as a *glocal public philosophy*. Only then can it incorporate the *Cosmopolitan dimension* into his relational ethics and, consequently, into the understanding of Self, Others, and the Public World.

3.1.3 From Hermeneutical Understanding of Self to Frustrated East Asian Public Philosophy: In the Case of Miki Kiyoshi (三木清 1897-1945)

As a very original philosopher deriving from Kyoto School, I would like now to take up Miki Kiyoshi, who, starting from a hermeneutical understanding of human beings in the last half of 1920s, developed his own public-philosophical thinking from the 1930s until his death in prison in 1945.[6]

Miki studied first under the guidance of Nishida at the University of Kyoto and then in Germany in the 1920s. He became influenced there first by Rickert and then by Heidegger and Dilthey, who fostered his intellectual interest in history both at the individual and global level. After he returned to Japan in 1925, he published *A Study on Human Being in Pascal* (1926). In this book, Miki interpreted Pascal's thought on the human being from the viewpoint of Heidegger (Miki [1980/1926]). Amazingly, this book was published one year before Heidegger's monumental book *Being and Time* (*Sein und Zeit*). Miki's starting point of thinking resembles Heidegger's hermeneutical ontology, but it was an original theory focusing on the human being who interprets and decides the pathway for his or her own mortal life. According to Miki, each Self is anxious about his or her death and can therefore develop each possibility in each living world. In this sense, the Self is understood as the *anxious, interpreting, and becoming Self.*

In essence, Miki did not abandon this existential viewpoint of the Self in his lifetime, as we will confirm later. At the same time, however, it must be stressed that this viewpoint of the Self was always understood in connection with the public world, characterized by its own historicity. The understanding of Self and Public World in Miki is united, and the *historicity of each Self* is always understood in relation to the public world; not only at the micro-level but also at the macro level *qua* world history. While Heidegger in *Sein und Zeit* regards the public world as a product of the inauthentic type of human being (*Das Man*), Miki regards it, on

[5] See Berque [2006].

[6] For an introduction to Miki written by a historian, see Townsend [2009].

the contrary, as a product of the Logos (reason and judgment) of the human being. He transformed Heideggerian categories such as *Sorge, Vorhabe, Vorsicht,* and *Vorgriff,* which are presupposed for each Self in understanding Self, Others, and World, into the public philosophical categories. The understanding of Self, Others, and Public World must relate to the historical consciousness of the present time in which each Self is living (Miki [1966-68/1928-39] Vol.3 pp. 186-220).

From this viewpoint, Miki began to be interested in philosophical Marxism, which was, at that time, represented by Fukumoto Kazuo (1894-1983), who studied in Germany under Lukacs and Korsch and became an influential ideologist in Japan. Fukumoto insisted on preparedness for philosophical arguments, engaging with the Communist Party as an avant-garde party. Although his radical ideology was rejected by Soviet-*Comintern* and he therefore had to retire from political commitment, Miki was stimulated by his thought and tried to interpret Marxism, especially its criticism of capitalism, in terms of his philosophy (ibid. pp. 1-156). This intellectual tendency is not parallel to that of other disciples of Nishida Kitaro. Miki had respected his teacher, Nishida, but abandoned Nishida's overly abstract thinking after he returned to Japan and began to teach at Hosei University in Tokyo. While Tanabe thus came near to Hegel's social or public philosophy after he criticized Nishida, Miki came near to "philosophical Marxism" and tried to reinterpret Marx via his own hermeneutical thinking.

This stance on Marxism related to Miki's commitment to journalistic activity. He contributed many columns to newspapers and can therefore be called a public intellectual. As I will describe in Chapter 4, the time of his activity was dark. *The Peace Preservation Law* was enforced in 1925, and many leftist activists were placed under arrest. Even Miki was arrested and imprisoned in 1930 after having financed the illegal Communist Party. After release from prison, he moderated his activity but never abandoned his commitment as a philosopher in journalism. When Heidegger joined the Nazis, Miki quickly criticized him. Reading his speech titled *Die Selbstbehauptung der deutschen Universität* (*the self-assertion of the German university*) in 1933, Miki pointed out that Nietzsche's thoughts on such topics as heroism, aristocratism, the glorifying of the Dionysian mind, and even war had had a bad influence on him (Miki Vol.10, pp. 310-320). Therefore, it became a serious task for Miki to overcome both "Logocentrism" that ignores the pathos in human beings and "Nihilism" that ignores the dignity of human beings.

From this experience, Miki attached much importance to *rhetoric as a means of communication*. As is well known, rhetoric was, together with ethics and politics, one of the most important elements in Aristotle's practical philosophy. Citing Aristotle's thought that credibility in rhetoric relies on the *Ethos* of the speaker, the *Pathos* of the listener, and *Logos* in speech itself, he emphasized that the rhetoric regarded as an art of persuasion is a practical integration of logic, ethics, and psychology. On the other hand, he criticized hermeneutics because it lacks thinking about the practice (Miki Vol.5 pp. 139-158). Unfortunately, Miki never knew the dialogical thinking of Gadamer's hermeneutics that appeared in the 1960s, and his criticism of hermeneutics was based upon Dilthey's (although Gadamer once met Miki in Germany).[7] While Watsuji left Dilthey's hermeneutics and instead developed a relational national ethics, Miki left Dilthey, as well as Heidegger, and instead developed his public activity in society based upon his own idea of rhetoric.

In this regard, it must be pointed out that Miki clearly distinguished the public who can form intellectual public judgment and opinion from the crowd or masses that have no solid public opinion. Since the second half of the 1930s, he criticized the loss of the public in this sense, as well as the loss of the public character of cultures such as the arts, science, and philosophy, and deplored especially the loss of the public mind of politics (Miki Vol.16. pp. 111-113, 115-117).

This is why Miki tried to commit himself to the brain trust called Showa Workshop for the Konoe Cabinet in 1937. To lay the philosophical foundation for this brain trust, Miki advocated a *Corporatism*, which always sides with the social public and opposes individualism, totalitarianism, materialism, and idealism. According to him, the corporatism first attaches much importance to public benefit or values and to the social practice of each individual, which makes it different from individualism. Second, it does not neglect the identity and spontaneity of each individual, which makes it different from forms of totalitarianism such as racism, nationalism, and Nazism. Third, it takes an epistemological realism that recognizes Others and Public World as autonomous beings, which makes it different from epistemological idealism and materialism. Fourth, it takes also an epistemological constructivism, which never accepts the status quo and always tries to reform the public world, which makes it different from epistemological conservatism (Miki Vol. 17 pp. 535-588).

It must be emphasized here that this idea is not confined to the national level. Miki tried to situate his corporatism in the world historical perspective at that time and regarded overcoming capitalism as its urgent task. For this task, he conceived *the East Asian Community* (東亜共同体), which consists mainly of China and Japan and seeks to cope with Western imperialism. In his study on the history of cultural exchange between Japan and China (published in English in 1941), Miki quoted from the speech Sun Wen made in Japan, 1924, and advocated the Corporation with China, which had been invaded by imperialistic Europe as well as Japan (ibid. pp. 181-184). This means also the attempt to overcome nationalism both in Japan and China without losing the national identity of both countries.

Indeed, this was Miki's' alternative to the Japanese imperialistic policy of

[7] See Gadamer [1960]. Gadamer recollected Miki as a former colleague; see Gadamer [1996].

those days. However, this idea was too idealistic to realize in such a hard situation and was destined to be frustrated; i.e., replaced by *The Greater East Asia Co-Prosperity Sphere* (大東亜共栄圏) put forward by the Japanese government in 1940. Miki had to retire from public activity and devoted himself to his philosophical studies such as *The Logic of the Power of Imagination* and *Essay on Shinran* (親鸞) (Miki Vol.18 pp.421ff), which were posthumous because he died as a political prisoner in 1945.

How do we appraise the legacy of Miki's philosophy?

First of all, I would like to say that Miki's attempt deserves to be classed as a public philosophy in all senses. His understanding of the word *public* was not the meaning of something relating to the state but of something relating to all the people; not only in Japan but also in other countries. In this sense, he might be called a *trans-national or glocal public philosopher*. Indeed, his thinking was not parallel to that of other philosophers in the Kyoto School. Second, his public philosophy always attempted to lay an ontological foundation, as his works from *A Study on Human Being in Pascal* in 1926 to *Logic of Imagination* shows. His Self was not the rational one but the one who tries to integrate *reason, passion, and responsibility* in each Self. He believed that only such integration could cope with the nihilism and crisis of his days. Unfortunately, he could not develop this rather *existential view of Self* alongside his *trans-national public philosophy* due to his death in prison. Therefore, it should be our task to develop his positive legacy in the present situation.

A Short Comment on the Failure of Overcoming Modernity by the Kyoto School

Now, I would like to take this opportunity to offer a critical comment on the ideology of *Overcoming Modernity*, expressed in 1942 by some Japanese intellectuals, to which I referred in Chapter 1.[8] This advocacy was announced in an interdisciplinary colloquium among representative philosophers, historians, and critics of those days. Neither Miki nor Tanabe took part in that event. It was Nishitani Keiji (西谷啓次 1900-90) as a distinguished young philosopher and Suzuki Narishige (鈴木成高 1907-1988) as a similarly distinguished young historian who enthusiastically advocated the ideology as children of the Kyoto School. Nishitani regarded modernity as a time of splitting between culture, history, and ethics, and a time of splitting between liberalism and nationalism. Suzuki formulated the targets of overcoming modernity as democracy in politics, capitalism in economy, and liberalism in social thought. He also made it their task to limit the role of the natural sciences and to overcome the conflict between progressivism and relativism in history. Both agreed that the Japanese should bear this task because they are the only people in Asia who are half westernized.

8 On this theme written in English, see Calichman [2008].

In my view, this advocacy itself may be half true so far as it was oriented against Western colonialism. Still, it remained fairly arrogant and even unrealistic because it was based on the total negligence of imperialistic behavior in other Asian countries. It lacked any respect for other cultures and histories in Asia, which Miki had shown (as described above). Therefore, it should be said that this attempt was not frustrated but also deceptive from the beginning.[9]

Now that I have reconsidered the negative and positive legacy of public philosophers deprived from the Kyoto School in the 1930s and 1940s, I will take up the representative public philosophers in post-WWII Japan.

3.2 Reappraisal of Representative Postwar Japanese Public Philosophies

As described in Chapter 1, Japan became a democratic country with a new constitution promulgated in 1947. The status of emperor was downgraded to a symbol of the state. Against this new background, a brand new trend of political and social thought appeared in Japan. Among others, I take up two influential thinkers from the University of Tokyo here.

3.2.1 National, International, and Christian Public Philosophy: In the Case of Nanbara Shigeru (南原繁 1989-1974)

Nanbara was the first president of the University of Tokyo in postwar Japan, and, as a leading public intellectual, he exerted a great influence on young people.[10] His thought was characterized by his rich knowledge of European political philosophy, as well as by his faith in Christianity based upon the *Non-church movement* in Japan. This movement began with Uchimura Kanzo (内村鑑三 1861-1930), who was a leading Christian intellectual in the Meiji and Taisho Era. Accordingly, Nanbara was consistently critical of State Shinto established in the Meiji Era. In the Empire of Japan, Shinto shrines were considered secular organs of the state, and this classification caused no serious opposition from the Japanese public. Hardly any philosophers derived from the Kyoto School criticized State Shinto. In such a prewar situation, Nanbara advocated his "Christian International public order," although he did so in an academic style.

In his major book *State and Religion*, published in 1942 during the war period, Nanbara not only criticized State Shinto but also any Hegelian idea of state that denies international public values beyond the state and justifies the war. He criticized Tanabe Hajime's *Logic of Species*, inspired by Hegel, as he saw that it amounted

9 My criticism of this attempt is harsher than Hiromatsu's critical appraisal [1989], which is described in this chapter.

10 On Nanbara as a public intellectual, see Barshay [1988] pp.35-122.

to a new justification of "State Religion." Instead of Hegelian public philosophy, he supported the Kantian idea of *Perpetual Peace* grounded on the "federation of peaceful states" as the world public order. Nanbara also highly estimated the Kantian moral philosophy that attaches much importance to the autonomy of each individual as a moral agency. Any religion must no longer neglect the dimension of autonomy of the individual, as Kant stressed (Nanbara [2014/1942] Chap. 3, pp. 149-236).

Nanbara did not, however, agree with Kantian Cosmopolitanism, which attaches little importance to the individual cultures of each nation. Citing cultural romanticism, he highlighted the need to respect the "uniqueness of each nation in terms of cultures." In this regard, Nanbara estimated Fiche more than Hegel in order to overcome Kantian cosmopolitanism, because Fichte includes both national and individual values, as his *Speech to the German Nation* (Fichte [1978/1808]) and *Study on Human Beatitude Based on the Gospel according to St. John* show (Fichte [2012/1806]).

Nanbara developed this *international and national* public philosophy in post-WWII Japan. It should be stressed that he made neither the conversion nor revision of thought that Tanabe and Watsuji formulated in this context (as described above). As a Kantian Christian, he believed that the ultimate purpose of politics is the realization of truth, goodness, and beauty. Against the totalitarian interpretation, he vindicated Fichte as a cultural nationalist of resistance (Nanbara [1959]). According to him, the democratic nation must rest on the independence of each individual to pursue freedom and peace, and post-WWII Japan should become an ethical nation with high cultural ideals. Though he was critical of Marxism, which had been very influential in post-WWII Japan, he emphasized the importance of the social rights and justice of the people. As for the emperor's responsibility for the war, he was of opinion that Emperor *Hirohito* should abdicate and that Akihito should become the new emperor as a symbol of a peaceful and moral Japanese nation (Nanbara Vol.9 pp. 98-108).

With regard to international relations, Nanbara maintained that Japan should play an independent moral role for world peace that relies on justice as the most important public value. With this thought, he was against the *San Francisco Peace Treaty* that was signed mainly by Western countries in 1951 and instead maintained the peace treaty with all belligerent nations, including China, India, the Soviet Union, etc.[11] Although this idea seems too idealistic to realize in view of the international situation of those days, Nanbara never considered himself an idealist but an *idealistic realist*. It was important for him that the search for ideal public order be pursued on the basis of understanding the social reality. In this regard, the

[11] This speech made Prime Minster Yoshida Shigeru so angry at the time that Yoshida called Nanbara a timeserving scholar.

Neo-Kantian distinction of *Being (Sein)* and *Ought To (Sollen)* cannot be abandoned, and the Hegelian synthesis of it must be rejected. The peace treaty with all the counties was for him not a utopia but an indispensable as well as realizable ideal (Nanbara Vol. 5 pp. 100-112). As a matter of fact, the *Japan-China Joint Statement* was announced in 1972 and had never been anticipated by the Japanese government in the 1950s and 60s.

Nanbara's interest was, however, not limited to political orders and values. He noticed the crisis of modern sciences caused by positivism, as well as overspecialization of knowledge, and advocated the significance of the humanities and liberal arts. According to him, the role of the humanities lies in making every scholar recognize how special forms of knowledge relate to one another and how each form is situated in the whole system of knowledge. Therefore, it is very important that every student and scholar learn the humanities not only 'before' he or she begins his or her special studies but also *after* he or she has learned his or her special studies (Nanbara Vol. 7. 161ff.). To realize this idea, Nanbara as president founded the *College of Arts and Sciences* for senior students at the University of Tokyo in 1951. In my view, this idea can be understood as a model precedent to our idea of the Post-specialization of Sciences advocated in the first chapter and developed in the other chapters.

What is the legacy of Nanbara's public philosophy?

The positive legacy is clear. First, in terms of political philosophy, Nanbara's public philosophy as *not only national but also international* must be noted. Though he specialized in European political philosophy, Nabara emphasized cooperation between Japan and other Asian countries; including red China. His support for the Kantian idea of international order should be appreciated, and his stance of an idealistic realist that has an affinity with the Rawlsian idea of *Realistic Utopia* could likewise be appreciated in today's international situation. Second, in terms of sciences and knowledge, his support of *interdisciplinary liberal arts* must be integrated into *our tripartite method of learning through interdisciplinary collaboration*, as was advanced in Chapter 2. We cannot doubt that Nanbara would accept our diagnosis, as so many *glocal* public issues in the world such as war and peace, nuclear weapons, nuclear energy, global warming, human rights, justice, poverty, wellbeing, etc., require public discussions and interdisciplinary collaborations.

What we miss in Nanbara's public philosophy is first the *ontology or theory of Self*. We can easily assume that his public philosophy presupposed a national and an international Self that corresponds well to our idea of a *multi-dimensional Self*. His public philosophy remains, however, blind to the minority people in Japan who do not have a national identity, such as Koreans or Chinese individuals. Second, it lacks the dimension of *civil society* that cannot be identified with national political society. Third, Nanbara's *idea of justice* as the most important public value remains too abstract to conceive. Fourth, he was too optimistic about the progress of *modern technological civilization*, although he was very critical of positivism. As a matter of fact, at the graduation ceremony of the University of Tokyo in 1947, he stated that nuclear power would usher in the second industrial revolution. This view was too uncritical of nuclear power, which we will discuss in Chapter 5. In sum, these insufficiencies are just what our *glocal* public philosophy must overcome.

3.2.2 Radical Individualistic and Democratic Thought for the Rehabilitation of Modernity: In the Case of Maruyama Masao (丸山眞男 1914-1996)

Maruyama, who was a disciple of Nanbara, exercised more influence on the young people than his teacher.[12] After being drafted into the Japanese army, he became a professor of Japanese political thought at the University of Tokyo. The trauma of his student days made him very critical of the mentality of Japanese Ultra-statism. According to him, the pre war political system that led Japan into the Second World War can be called the *System of Irresponsibility* (Maruyama [1967/1957-1958], [2008/1963]). In order to break down this system, it is very important for the postwar Japanese people to combine radical individualism with radical democracy, which should be regarded as an unfinished task. Based upon this idea, Maruyama has been a public philosopher both as an academic scholar and an eminent public intellectual in the press circle.

Maruyama's thought was characterized by his modern *dualism of nature (cosmos) and invention (nomos)*. In his maiden work, *Studies in the Intellectual History of Tokugawa Japan*, Maruyama introduced this dualism in a positive way. According to him, Neo-Confucianism in Tokugawa Japan identified the governmental code with the natural order, while the Confucianism of Ogyu Sorai (荻生徂徠 1666-1728) regarded the governmental code as an invention by human beings. As a result, the former played the role of uncritically affirming feudal public order; the latter showed a way to relativize the feudal public order. In this sense, Sorai was a forerunner of modern thinking on public order in Japan, though he remained in Confucianism (Maruyama [1995-96 Vol.3/1941], [2008/1974]).

Based upon this view, Maruyama interpreted the modern history of Japan since the Meiji era. He regarded the *Movement for Freedom and People's Rights* from the 1870s until the 1880s as the decisive movement for the invention of public order. As for Fukuzawa Yukichi, who I have mentioned in Chapter 1 and will take up in next chapter, Maruyama highly estimated him as a modern enlightenment thinker, as well as a sound nationalist (Maruyama [2001/1942-1992]). He believed

[12] There are many studies on Maruyama; not only in a Japanese context but also on an international scale. However, I do not refer to them here.

that the Ultra-statism in prewar Japan occurred because the development of sound nationalism that Fukuzawa had once advocated was frustrated.[13]

Democracy can be strongest when the people consistently supervise and criticize institutions. The people, however, consist of individuals, not all of whom are necessarily political. In this regard, Maruyama attached much importance to non-political citizens as supporters of democracy that must always be innovated. He classified individualism into two categories; i.e., one that is oriented toward "atomization or privatization" and the other that is oriented toward "independence or democratization." Of course, he criticized the former and supported the latter (Maruyama [1965]).

As for the Japanese New Constitution, he situated it in the historical context, as Article 97 proclaims:

> The fundamental human rights by this Constitution guaranteed to the people of Japan are the fruits of the age-old struggle of man to be free; they have survived the many exacting tests for durability and are conferred upon this and future generations in trust, to be held for all time inviolate.

Its cardinal ideas are human rights and perpetual peace. It was the radical individualism and democracy that support and put these ideas into practice. As for Article 9, this states:

> Aspiring sincerely to an international peace based on justice and order, the Japanese people forever renounce war as a sovereign right of the nation and the threat or use of force as means of setting international disputes.
>
> In order to accomplish the aim of the preceding paragraph, land, sea, and air forces, as well as other war potential, will never be maintained. The right of belligerency of the state will not be recognized.

The Preamble also declares:

> We, the Japanese people, desire peace for all time and are deeply conscious of the high ideals controlling human relationship and we have determined to preserve our security and existence, trusting in the justice and faith of the peace-loving peoples of the world. We desire to occupy an honored place in an international society striving for the preservation of peace, and the banishment of tyranny and slavery, oppression and intolerance for all time from the earth. We recognize that all peoples of the world have the right to live in peace, free from fear and want.
>
> (http://www.solon.org/Constitutions/Japan/English/english-Constitution.html)

Maruyama believed that international peace should not rely upon power politics but should presuppose the international image of orientation toward the banish-

[13] It must be pointed out that there are some Japanese scholars who criticized Maruyama's positive appreciation of Fukuzawa.

ment of tyranny and slavery. He also interpreted the *right to live in peace, free from fear and want* as the development of the philosophy of peace advocated by Saint-Pierre, Kant, Gandhi, Yokoi Shonan, Ueki Emori, Uchimura Kanzo, and others (Maruyama [1982] pp. 39-50). Regarding the Japan Self-Defense Force established in 1954, he was of the opinion that it must be oriented from the viewpoint of reduction in armament. He emphasized the significance of August 15 as the anniversary of the end of the war, when Japan abandoned the military state and, paradoxically, became a leader of World Peace (Maruyama ibid. pp. 54-68).

As for his view of the university and sciences, he criticized the overspecialized department structure of the university as a type of octopus pot, instead emphasizing the significance of the university that has a common root and upon which any special sciences rest (Maruyama [1961] pp. 129-138). He also tried to advocate that every student should learn history and philosophy after they had learned their special sciences, but this was in vain (Maruyama [2006] pp. 272ff.). As an eminent scholar of the faculty of law, he was attacked by the extreme leftist student rioters at the end of 1960s and left the university.

How should we appraise Maruyama's achievements?

First of all, it is doubtless that his commitment to the public world in post-WWII Japan deserves appreciation. In my view, his critique of the system of irresponsibility in Japanese organizations remains valid, as the recent human-made disaster of the nuclear power plant accident in Fukushima shows. In this sense, Maruyama's public philosophy has been never obsolete. His critique of the overspecialized department system of universities and the abovementioned plan for the reorientation of philosophy and history should also be taken up for our idea of a post-specialized *glocal* public philosophy.

Nevertheless, I have to point out Maruyama's philosophical shortcomings. He did not abandon his *dualistic viewpoints of nature and invention*. However, this quasi-Cartesian or Kantian dualism must be radically modified in face of today's ecological crisis. In other words, we must now think that the human being belongs to nature, or, ontologically speaking, the Self and Others are both mental as well as natural beings, and *the public world includes nature as the ecological world*. Therefore, his modernistic dualism must be replaced with ecological thinking and ecological democracy. As for the minority people in Japan who do not have a national identity, Maruyama seems not have been as sensitive as Nanbara. Maruyama was not interested in the new normative political theory that Rawls, Habermas, and others had been developing since the 1970s.[14] Therefore, he could not lay a philosophical foundation for *bridging the radical individualism and democracy* that he advocated. It could be the case that radical individualism would combine with fascism or anti-democracy. In this regard, I have to say that Maruyama's political

[14] Maruyama seems not have read Rawls [1971] and Habermas [1981] sincerely.

thought remains on the level of the so-called political Dezisionismus.[15] It may be our task to overcome these insufficiencies.

3.3 Other Prominent Public Philosophies in Postwar Japan

Now, I will shed light on the legacy of some other public philosophies in postwar Japan.

3.3.1 The Legacy of the Comparative Religious Philosophy of Nakamura Hajime (中村元1912-1999) and Izutsu Toshihiko (井筒俊彦 1914-1993)

What I would like to take up here is the legacy of comparative religious philosophy in postwar Japan, and, among others, that of Nakamura Hajime and Izutsu Toshihiko. While postwar public philosophers such as Nanbara and Maruyama showed strongly modernistic traits, both philosophers tried to relativize modern Western philosophies and open new perspectives in terms of comparative philosophy on a worldwide level.

a) The Public Philosophical Aspects of Nakamura Hajime's Thought

Nakamura was an internationally known Buddhist philosopher. As an expert on Sanskrit and Pali, he translated many Buddhist scriptures into Japanese, but he was not satisfied with the immanent interpretation of Buddhism and tried to reinterpret the contemporary significance of Buddhism for the people. Further, he enthusiastically advanced the comparative philosophy from the perspective of world civilization (Nakamura [1964]).

According to Nakamura, realizing the truth in Buddhism means the realization of the true Self in relationship to Others and, therefore, to mutual aids. The principle of action to realize this truth is *Jihi* (慈悲 maitreya), which means both friendship and deep compassion (Nakamura [2010/1955]). This principle must be understood as universal love and peace among the people, independent of any religions and nations, and social institutions must follow this principle as far as possible. Pointing out the historical fact that there was no death penalty in the *Heian Period* (平安時代 pp. 794-1192), he criticized the policy of severe punishment (Nakamura [2004] pp. 174ff.). Nakamura rejected sectionalism in Buddhism and insisted that any religion must be relativized. All statesmen and people should learn from *Asoka* (263-232 B.C.) in India, who supported freedom of faith (though he was a Buddhist), preached the peaceful co-existence of all religions, and even advocated cooperation among them in order to realize truth and peace both in the

15 What I mean by Dezisionismus here is the idea that politics does not rely upon normative theories but only upon the decisions of politicians or people.

world and in the mind (*nirvana*) (Nakamura [1985] Chap. 7-12). Nakamura emphasized the cosmopolitan character of Buddhism and showed his sympathy with the idea of world-federation (ibid. Chap. 13).

Thus, in my view, Nakamura's thought can be regarded as a promising Buddhist *glocal* public philosophy for the future. It remains to be seen how someone else who is deeply versed in Buddhist thought develops his interesting legacy.

b) The Case of Izutsu Toshihiko

Another comparative religious philosopher I would like to take up is Izutshu Toshihiko, who once taught at McGill University in Canada, as well as at the *Iran Royal Academy of Philosophy*. He published a lucid introduction to Islamic culture for Japanese readers (Izutsu [1991/1981]), but his main intellectual interest was to raise the universality of mystical thought to the level of logos through the comparative study of Islam and Eastern thought; especially Taoism and Zen Buddhism. In his great work published in 1983, *Consciousness and Substance – Searching for the Spiritual East*, he was seeking a point that would comprehend the substance of things; not only on the surface of consciousness, which appears in the mere indicative function of language, but the Being of Self, Others, and World on the level of deep consciousness (Izutsu [1983]).

In order to overcome many present civilization crises, Izutsu used this ontological basis to advocate dialog between the Western modern worldview that requires innovation and the Eastern philosophy that had long traditions spanning more than a hundred years. This project requires what H. G. Gadamer calls the *fusion of horizons* and the accumulation of many dialogs. Izutsu made it a Japanese mission to induce European, Chinese, Indian, and Islamic philosophies to confront one another (Izutsu [1992] pp. 11-43, 263-307).

In my view, this mission corresponds with the *Dialog among Civilizations* advocated by the ex-president of Iran, Seyyed Mohammad Khatami, as a counterview of the Clash of Civilization described by Samuel Hungtington.[16] What I miss, however, is the lack of political or social ethical dimension in Izutu's thought, as he himself admitted. It would be necessary for the dialog of civilization to consider public values such as human rights, peace, etc., and negative values such as political suppression, war, poverty, terrorism, etc. To develop his rich ontological thought, I suggest that the ideas of *glocal* public philosophy should be introduced.

3.3.2 The Legacy of Neo-Marxism: In the Case of Hiromatsu Wataru (廣松渉 1933-1994)

In prewar Japan, especially since the 1930s, the promotion and study of Marxism had been officially prohibited. In such a situation, Tosaka Jun (戸坂潤 1900-1945)

[16] The idea of Dialog among Civilizations once influenced UNESCO.

supported dialectical Marxism and published many books and articles. Unfortunately, he was arrested and died in prison in1945, as did Miki Kiyoshi.

In post-WWII Japan, philosophical as well as political Marxism became a major trend and exerted a great influence on young students until the 1960s.[17][18] This trend, however, declined rapidly from the 1970s onwards, although non-philosophical-Marxists such as Uchida Yoshihiko (内田義彦 1913-1989) and Hirata Kiyoaki (平田清明 1922-1995) advocated the civil-society against orthodox Marxist-Leninism (which I will discuss in Chapter 4). In terms of philosophy, however, the legacy of one Neo-Marxist since the 1970s deserves to be considered. His name is Hiromatsu Wataru, and he wrote numerous books that attracted the attention of not only leftist students and intellectuals but non-leftist students and intellectuals. Some of his books were also translated into Chinese.

Emphasizing his task of overcoming the Cartesian dualistic worldview, Hiromatsu attempted to innovate the philosophical heritage of Marxism by opposing it to the various philosophical tendencies of the 20th century. On a fundamental level, he criticized the modern worldview, whether idealistic or materialistic, that was caught in the dualistic grid of subject and object. He rejected the Leninist type of materialistic theory, which sees in the object the mere product of reflection of matter. Instead, he developed a new theory that recognizes the object as the intersubjectively constituted world of relation (Hiromatsu [1991], [1996/1993]). In the background of this kind of thinking, one can detect the strong influence of constitutionalism derived from phenomenology and Neo-Kantianism; especially the relationalistic epistemology of E. Cassirer. Still, Hiromatsu always placed his philosophical activity at the center of the Marxist tradition in that he considered the world of relations not as an a priori trans-historical world but as an a posteriori socio-historical world, which is in constant need of reform or even revolution (Hiromatsu ibid.).

In *Being and Meaning,* Hiromatsu tries to explain the genesis of intersubjective recognition of values in terms of the social role of each individual as *Becoming Self* and *Others*. According to him, each Self recognizes social or public values by co-operating with other members of society and then developing his or her worldview. The goal of such dynamic development of Self, Others, and World is a realization of the just public world on the basis of social justice (Hiromatsu [1996 Vol.16] p.484). This project corresponds partly to the overcoming of modernity. As a matter of fact, Hiromatsu paid much attention to the failure of the Kyoto School's attempt (as described above) and wrote a monograph on this subject (Hiromatsu [1989]). He evaluated such attempts, especially Suzuki Narishige's, to

17 On Marxism in postwar Japan, see Piovesana [1997] pp.207-218.

18 The author (Yamawaki [1997] pp.271-273) once appreciated Hiromatsu as a Japanese original Marxist in the 1980s.

some extent, which stands in contrast to Nanbara and Maruyama. Naturally, as a Marxist philosopher, he criticized the poor knowledge of capitalism and historical realities of the Kyoto School (ibid. Chap. 10).

How do we estimate Hiromatsu's legacy? On the one hand, I admit that his ontological as well as epistemological understanding of Self, Others, and Public World bears a close parallel to our idea of *multidimensional, responsive-becoming Self, Others, and Public World*. While the modernistic public philosophy of Nanbara and Maruyama refrained from developing philosophical ontology, Hiromatsu enthusiastically committed himself to it and attempted to overcome modernity. We have to estimate his efforts in this respect positively. Still, we have to point out his astonishing lack of *political* public philosophy, although he considered himself a new type of Marxist. Just before his death due to illness, he contributed a very controversial article to *Asahi Newspaper* and advocated the establishment of a new East Asian public order from the left wing (Hiromatsu [1996/1994] Vol.14 pp.497-500). It is nice as an idea, to be sure, but he could not develop his strategy for its realization. Speaking more critically, his understanding of democracy and human rights as political or public values remained unclear. If we should revive the positive legacy of Hiromatsu, we would have to discard his attachment to Marxism and retain his rich ontological thinking about the *Becoming Self, Others, and the Public World*.

4 Developments of Ideas on Democracy and Civil Society in Japan from a Perspective of *Glocal* Public Philosophy*

In this chapter, I will reflect on the developments of ideas on democracy and civil society in modern Japan from the perspective of *glocal* public philosophy formulated in the previous chapters. This reflection is necessary and very important; especially because modern Japan was the first Asian country that not only established parliamentary democracy as a *positive* legacy, but, at the same time, entered into the colonial Western powers, which can be seen as a *negative* legacy in modern Japan.

Departing from this concern, I will reflect on the historical developments of ideas on *democracy* in modern Japan as Part I (4.1). Then, I will reflect on the historical development of ideas on *civil society* both in *Japan* and *Germany* (4.2).

On the basis of these reflections, I would like to conceive the possibility of *trans-national democracy and civil society* in which we should make efforts to promote trans-national public values, as well as dispose of trans-national negative values (4.3).

Part I

4.1 Reflections on the Development of Ideas on Democracy in Modern Japan

In this first part, I discuss the development of ideas on democracy in modern Japan by classifying three phases, which correspond to each historical background.

4.1.1 From the Movement for Freedom and People's Rights to the End of the Meiji Period as the First Phase (1868-1912)

I will now begin to describe the so-called *Movement for Freedom and People's Rights* from the 1870s until the 1880s. As was shown already in Chapter 1, Japan's modernization began with the Meiji Restoration in 1868 when the new emperor

---

* This chapter is largely a modified version of my article written in German (Yamawaki [2013]).

replaced the Tokugawa shogunate, the feudal status was abolished, and the construction of an integrated national polity began.[1]

In March of 1868, the new government proclaimed a *Five-Article Oath under the name of Emperor (Tennō)*, which was drafted by Yuri Kimimasa (由利公正 1829-1909): a disciple of Yokoi Shōnan (横井小楠 1809-1869). As I described in Chapter 1, Yokoi was influenced by a Neo-Confucian thought: "the Universal Public Principle (Logos) of Heaven and Earth" (天地公共の実理). He considered the ultimate legitimacy of politics to lie in the "public discussion of the Japanese people" (公論、公議), and he believed that Japan could become a more virtuous country through this approach. In my view, Yuri was more or less influenced by Yokoi's thought.

The Five-Article Oath drafted by Yuri and others was expressed as follows.

1. Deliberative assemblies shall be widely established and all matters decided by public discussion.
2. All classes, high and low, shall unite in vigorously carrying out the administration of affairs of the state.
3. The common people, no less than civil and military officials, shall be allowed to pursue their own individual callings so that there may be no discontent.
4. Evil customs of the past shall be broken off and everything based upon the just law of nature.
5. Knowledge shall be sought throughout the world so as to strengthen the foundations of imperial rule.[2]

Indeed, it was against the background of these articles that the so-called *Movement for Freedom and People's Rights* occurred from the 1870s until the 1880s. Encouraged by public discussion, as well as the equality of the Japanese nation declared in the oath, this movement managed to establish some modern political systems such as parliamentary government. At the same time, however, Japan established the imperial public order. I will now discuss several public intellectuals in this period.

a) *Radical Thinkers in this Movement – Nakae Chōmin (中江兆民 1847-1901) and Ueki Emori (植木枝盛 1859-1892)*

It should be noted that most important modern European ideas were translated into Japanese during this time. As for political philosophy, the important works of J.S. Mill and J.J. Rousseau were translated and introduced by the representative thinkers in this movement. *Nakamura Masanao* (中村正直 1832-1891), who started his career as a Confucian and converted to Christianity after studying in

[1] For an excellent and detailed study on the modern history of Japan, see Gordon [2013].

[2] ibid. p.78.

England, translated Mill's *On Liberty* into Japanese and encouraged young students to participate in this movement.

A more famous public philosopher than Nakamura was *Nakae Chōmin,* who studied in France, translated a part of Rousseau's *Du contrat social* into Japanese, and urged the government to recognize the radical right of the people. Influenced not only by Rousseau but by also Mencius (孟子), he criticized the utilitarian hedonistic idea of public welfare and instead emphasized the significance of the "liberte morale" of each individual, arguing that this lays the foundation for human rights and democracy (Nakae [1984/1882-1901] pp. 63-135). As a political system, however, he did not advocate direct democracy in the manner of Rousseau but rather *governance by the emperor and the Japanese people*, which resembles constitutional monarchy in England. In this regard, his political ideas seem to have stood between Rousseau and Mill, although he never accepted utilitarian ideas.

Regarding international relations, Nakae published a very famous book, *A Discourse by Three Drunkards on Government*, in 1887, which was translated into both English and French.[3] In this book, three persons – a "nationalistic-expansionistic Champion," who advocates the policy of increasing military strength, a "westernized Gentleman," who advocates the policy of unarmed neutrality, and "modest Professor Nankai," who advocates the policy of gradual social reform under a realistic insight into international relations – are discussing their vision of Japanese politics. Although Nakae does not favor any person and instead leaves judgment to the readers, he seems to support the modest Professor Nankai (Nakae [1965/1887]).

Against these intellectual backgrounds, Nakae not only wielded a powerful pen as a militant journalist but also committed himself to "Realpolitik" as a member of parliament. His efforts were frustrated, however, and he plunged into his private enterprise and philosophical speculation on a materialistic worldview in his later years (Nakae [1984/1882-1901] pp. 353ff.).

In my view, the most radical democratic thinker in this movement was arguably *Ueki Emori*. Unlike Nakae, Ueki never studied abroad but researched many modern western political ideas intensively by himself and developed them in his own way. As a radical thinker, he harshly criticized "Burke's conservatism" and its denial of natural rights, and he consequently developed natural rights ideas for human beings. He drafted a constitution in which radical ideas such as the abolishment of patriarchy, the equality of the sexes and even the rights of children, the decentralization of power, and so forth, were declared. Regarding international relations, Ueki criticized European colonialism and emphasized the need for solidarity with Asian countries for their independence. Moreover, he advocated reducing

[3] For an English translation of this work, see Nakae [1984/1887]; for a French translation, see Nakae [2008/1887].

armament and the formation of a kind of World Federation of Nations for this purpose (Ueki [1990/1879-91]). His ideas were, however, too radical to be accepted in his days. He died or was assassinated at the age of 33 and fell into oblivion

b) Liberal-National Public Philosopher – Fukuzawa Yukichi (福沢諭吉 1835-1901)

This democratic movement resulted in frustration, however, because the *Meiji Constitution,* which was modeled after the "Prussian Constitution" and promulgated in 1889, declared the *imperial (emperor's) sovereignty*. Although this constitution endorsed some modern political systems such as "parliamentary government and plural party systems" that can be regarded as outcomes of the movement, there is no denying that it brought the first phase of democracy in Japan to an end. After that, the nationalistic as well as expansionist tendency became stronger and stronger in order to cope with the European powers of those days.

Even the liberal enlightened thinkers began to be involved in this tendency. To clarify this line of thought, I would like to turn again to *Fukuzawa Yukichi* (福沢諭吉), who visited US and European countries in his younger days and became one of the most popular modern enlightened public philosophers in Japan.

As I demonstrated in Chapter 1, Fukuzawa was of the opinion that the independence of each individual as a private person would enable a nation-state to be independent. He declared in his million-selling *An Encouragement of Learning* that all persons are born equal and there is no hierarchy among them. The difference among persons depends on the degree to which each individual becomes learned. Unlike Yokoi and Nakae, he had no sympathy with Confucian ideas in general and instead admired Western ideas. According to him, there is only a government and no nation in Japan, and the foundation of the Japanese nation should be realized by the power of individuals who have mastered the art of learning (Fukuzawa [1978/1872-76], [1963/1872-76]).

Fukuzawa's liberal public philosophy had a clear limitation, however, as is evidenced when we shed light on his "international idea." Fukuzawa, who had been strongly influenced by the French historian and politician François Guizot (1787-1874), believed that proof of degree of civilization lies in state-sovereignty. Consequently, he intended to establish a state-sovereignty in Japan that would be just as strong as that seen in European powers (Fukuzawa [1995/1875], [1973/1875] Chap. 10). To be sure, he was right in wanting to emancipate Japanese people from a dependency on European power. However, it must be pointed out that the European powers of his day such as England, France, Germany, etc., were colonial nation-states. As was shown in Chapter 1, after the breakdown of the revolutionary project led by Kim Ok-kyun (金玉均 1851-1894) in Korea, he lost interest not only in China but also in Korea. From a *glocal* viewpoint, his liberal and national public philosophy did not offer any critical viewpoint against the colonialist international order to which the Japanese state began to commit itself.[4]

c) Local-Ecological Public Philosopher – Tanaka Shōzō (田中正造 1841-1913)

In spite of this nationalistic fade-out of democracy, the public activities and original ideas of *Tanaka Shōzō*, whose philosophy forms a sharp contrast with that of Fukuzawa, should be appreciated here. What had made Tanaka Shōzō famous was his direct petition as a Diet member to the emperor for the relief of the people suffering from pollution caused by "Ashio Copper Mine" (足尾銅山) in the Tochigi prefecture (Tanaka [2004/1879-1903]). Although this attempt failed in 1901, the media reported the incident on a large scale, and, as a result, a large donation for the suffering people was collected from all over the Japan.

Tanaka's significance lies especially in his later activities and ideas in a small village near Ashio Copper Mine. He criticized the centralistic modernization that the Meiji government had been promoting, and, instead, emphasized the public governance that both local political leaders and residents perform. He called such governance *Public Cooperation with Mutual Love* (公共協力相愛) (Tanaka [1979/1904-1913] pp.391-392). With this idea, he had been protesting against the abandonment of Taninaka village as decided by central government (Tanaka [2005/1904-13]).

It should be pointed out that this idea was produced from Tanaka's devotion to the idea of "benevolence" in Confucianism, as well as "Agape" in Christianity. Moreover, Tanaka praised the *ecological life of people* who live together with nature and criticized the project of industrialization led by the central government, which did not take environmental or natural destruction into account. In this regard, he esteemed the "pre-modern view of nature" that does not separate human being as subject from nature as object. In this regard, he could be seen as the most important *ecological public philosopher*, who paid much attention to environmental justice and human rights.

As for international politics, Tanaka denied any kind of war and advocated the disarmament of all countries. His last aphorism stated in 1912 is "genuine civilization does not destruct any mountains, any rivers, or any villages, and it never kills anyone." This aphorism must be revived today; especially because Minamata disease and the Fukushima nuclear plant accident as *glocal* cases betrayed it.[5]

---

4 In this sense, Fukuzawa took over not only the positive but also the *negative* legacy of modern Europe.

5 For excellent studies on Tanaka as an ecological public philosopher, see Komatsu [2011], [2013].

d) Trans-national Activist and Thinker – Miyazaki Tōten (宮崎滔天 1871-1922)

If we reflect on the relationship to Asia during this time, we have to re-appreciate *Miyazaki Tōten* as the most important *trans-national thinker and activist* of those days.

Miyazaki advocated solidarity against Western colonialism with revolutionary China and had a close connection with Chinese activists; especially Sun Wen (孫文 1866-1925). With this lofty ideal, he made also positive approaches to some other Chinese intellectuals. For example, he came to know Kang Youwei (康有為 1858-1927), who had failed to reform the Qing or Ching Dynasty as a Confucian reformist and had to take refuge in Hong Kong. Tōten subsequently brought Kang to Japan in 1898. It was a very interesting attempt on the part of Miyazaki to seek to make Sun a democratic revolutionist ally, with Kang as a Confucian reformer who stayed in Singapore.

Unfortunately, however, Miyazaki was confounded with an assassin and expelled from Singapore. He then came to Hong Kong, but he was expelled there as well. Still, this failed attempt had exerted a certain influence upon such reformists as Liang Qichao (梁啓超 1873-1929), who studied many subjects in Japan and created new Chinese words. It was against this frustrated background that Miyazaki's autography *My Thirty-Three Years' Dream* was published in 1903.[6] The abridged translation of this autobiography in Chinese was soon published under the title of *Sun-Yat-sen*, and Sun's name as a revolutionist became popular among the Chinese people (Miyazaki [1993/1902]).

Thus, Miyazaki could be called a *pro-China glocal activist*, but the resource of his activity was not Marxism or Confucianism but Christianity. In his later days, he became a supporter of *Taishō democracy*, which I describe next.

4.1.2 Ideas in Taishō Imperial Democracy as the Second Phase (1912-1930)

The second phase of democracy flourished mainly in the Taishō period (1912-1926) and is therefore called *Taishō Democracy*. This Taishō Democracy, however, developed in the context of the imperial Japan of those days, which had held colonial control of Taiwan since 1895 and Korea since 1910. In this sense, it might be called *imperial democracy* (to use the terminology of famous historian Andrew Gordon).[7] On the domestic level, the important political outcomes of Taishō Democracy were the Party Cabinet, which has existed since 1918, and the establishment of universal male suffrage in 1925.

[6] For an English translation of this work, see Miyazaki [1982/1902].

[7] See Gordon [2013] Part 3, pp. 138ff.

a) *The Quasi-Hegelian Idea of Minponshugi (民本主義) – Yoshino Sakuzō (吉野作造 1878-1933)*

The most famous democratic idea in this period was represented by *Yoshino Sakuzō*, who I have already described in Chapter 1.1. Regarding Taishō Democracy as *a development of Movement for Freedom and People's Rights in the Meiji period*, he advocated in 1916 the idea of constitutional politics and political systems "rooted in the people" (Minponshugi 民本主義). He intentionally avoided using the term "democracy" (Minshushugi 民主主義), because it could be associated with Rousseau's theory of general will and conflict with the existence of the emperor. He thought that it is Minponshugi that is compatible with both constitutional monarchy and representative democracy (Yoshino [1984/1914-1933] pp. 65-180). Yoshino was inspired by Hegel's ideas of cooperation between policymakers such as governmental officials and political parties entrusted by the Japanese people. He also studied the "modern history of China" intensively, focusing especially on revolutions, and he admired *Tōten's works* and activity. He tried to vindicate the protest movement of the Chinese students against feudalism and Japanese imperialism, which broke out on May 4, 1919, because it aimed for freedom and Minponshugi (民本主義) (ibid. pp. 221-241).

Universalizing a Hegelian progressive and Euro-centric view of history, he considered the victory of Japan over Russia, as well as the revolution of China in 1911, a victory of freedom over despotism. As a matter of fact, Yoshino studied in England, Germany, France, and the US before the First World War, and stayed in the Chinese mainland during the war. In this regard, he had been maintaining a *glocal viewpoint*. Indeed, he was not so radical as to claim to abolish the Japanese colonial policy that had existed in Korea since 1910, and this seemingly shows his limits of thinking. It should not be forgotten, however, that he was very critical of the assimilation policy that was in place during those days and that neglected the cultural identity of the Korean nation (ibid. pp. 241-259).[8]

b) *Other Eminent Thinkers – Fukuda Tokuzō (福田徳三 1874-1930) and Ishibashi Tanzan (石橋湛山 1884-1973)*

The democratic thought of the *Taishō* period was also represented by the economic philosopher *Fukuda Tokuzō* as a promoter of Taishō Democracy, together with Yoshino Sakuzō. Fukada's intellectual background was *the Japanese Association for Social Policy*, modeled after that in Germany. He had once studied in München under the guidance of L. Brentano, who represented the "left wing of the German Association for Social Policy." Stimulated by his thought, Fukuda advocated "democratic science" as a mode of social policy, meaning that each person struggles for the right to live and that the government approves this (Fukuda

[8] For a recent very comprehensive and excellent historical study on Yoshino, see Jung-Sun [2012].

[2015/1922]). He made great efforts to rebuild the downtown area after the "Great Kantō Earthquake" in 1923. He also criticized the abstract welfare economics represented by Alfred Marshall and A. C. Pigou in England because it remains on the level of price economics, and he thus integrated it into democratic science (Fukuda [1980/1930]). In today's world, this idea could be called democratic governance for the wellbeing of the people. As for his idea of the (civil) society as distinct from the state, I will take this up again in 4.2.

In the context of Taishō Democracy, the ideas of *Ishibashi Tanzan* also deserve to be re-appreciated. As an independent journalist, as well as a radical liberal, he supported democracy and the emancipation of women. From a *glocal* viewpoint, based upon his own liberal economic idea, he advocated *the Small Japan against the Great Japan* and the abandonment of colonialism, which Japan had been promoting not only in Taiwan and Korea but also in the Chinese mainland *Manchuria* (Ishibashi [1984/1912-1968]). In this regard, Ishibashi was more radical than Yoshino. In addition, as an influential statesman, he made great efforts after WWII to re-establish diplomatic relations with China's mainland and became a prime minister in the liberal-democratic cabinet (in 1956), though he resigned soon after due to illness.

The liberal-democratic thought of Yoshino, Fukuda, and Ishibashi was, however, frustrated in the 1930s, during which time Japan made a mad dash for invasion into China. The Taishō Democracy was changed into a kind of fascism in which liberal interpretation of Meiji Constitution was suppressed and the emperor's despotism became more and more dominant.

4.1.3 The Dark Side of the Modernization of Japan as a Negative Legacy

On this occasion, several dark historical events in this era should be mentioned.

The first event began with the *High Treason Incident* (大逆事件), just before the Taishō Era in 1910-11, as the first political oppression of leftist thinkers. Japanese police arrested many socialists and anarchists in 1910 on the pretext that they had attempted to assassinate the emperor. Although this pretext was groundless, the Japanese Supreme Court sentenced 24 defendants to death without calling any witnesses, and 12 of these persons were executed the next year. The most famous unjustly accused individual was *Kōtoku Shūsui* (幸徳秋水 1871-1911), who was a disciple of Nakae Chōmin (mentioned above) and later became an anarchist.[9] This event shocked the world and could therefore be called a *glocal* tragic event.

The political suppression of Japanese leftist thinkers reoccurred on the occasion of the Kantō Great Earthquake in 1923. Half a month after this earthquake, *Ōsugi Sakae* (大杉栄 1885-1923), who translated Kropotkin's *Mutual Aid* and

[9] For Kōtoku's work in French, see Kōtoku [2008/1901].

published several books from the viewpoint of a solidaristic anarchist, was killed, together with his wife and child, by the police. In 1925, while a law of universal suffrage for Japanese men was established, the notorious Peace Preservation Law that aimed at the political suppression of communists, socialists, and anarchists was enacted. This law was strengthened in 1928 and enabled the Special High Police, which was founded on the occasion of the abovementioned High Treason incident, to arrest many intellectuals.

The second dark historical event concerned Korean people's presence in Japan, as well as in the colonial Korean mainland. Since Japan annexed Korea as a colony in 1910, migration of Korean people has been increasing, and the Korean population in Japan amounted to more than 400,000 by 1930. Though they were regarded as Japanese subjects, they suffered from discrimination and prejudice. It was a scandal and tragedy that Japanese police and military troops killed several thousand Koreans at the time of the Kantō Great Earthquake (1923). Nevertheless, migration in search of jobs continued to increase, and the number of Korean people in Japan amounted to more than 2,000,000 at the end of WWII.

In the Korean mainland, the Japanese government imposed a cultural imperialism upon Korean people, forcing them to become Japanese subjects. They were also compelled to speak Japanese in schools and official places, as well as to change their Korean names to Japanese names (創氏改名). Moreover, the young Korean people were mobilized as Japanese members of the armed forces during World War Two. The case experience of Taiwanese people from 1895 to 1945 was similar to that of Korean people. This dark historical event could be also regarded as a *glocal* dark event that must not be forgotten.

As I criticized in the previous chapters, in such a situation, nothing was as deceptive as the ideology of *The Greater East Asia Co-Prosperity Sphere* put forward by the Japanese government in 1940, because the reality in East Asia was by no means of a co-prosperous nature. Rather, it was merely imperialistic in nature, as evidenced by the policy by which Japan forced East Asian peoples to speak Japanese in their countries' schools.

Thus, the period of the so-called 15 Year War between 1931 and 1945 was characterized as a fascistic period in which not only leftist ideas but also any democratic ideas were politically suppressed. In this sense, the philosophical efforts of Tanabe, Watsuji, and Miki that I discussed in the previous chapter must be critically reinterpreted and partly appreciated.

4.1.4 Postwar Democratic Thought as the Third Phase and New Task of Trans-national Democracy

As I have stated repeatedly, Japan became a democratic country with a new constitution. To be sure, Japan has maintained a good relationship with the US and Western Europe. Its relationship with East Asian countries, however, remains strained, although the Treaty on Basic Relations between Japan and the Republic of Korea was finalized in 1965, and the Japan-China Treaty of Peace and Friendship was finalized in 1978.

In the previous chapter, I discussed the thought of Nanbara and Maruyama as two representative post-WWII democratic public philosophers. Now, I once again take up their significance and limits for postwar democracy in Japan.

Indeed, Nanbara and Maruyama were representative founding fathers of post-war democratic Japan. As a Kantian-Fichtean Christian, Nanbara believed that the ultimate purpose of politics is the realization of truth, goodness, and beauty. Against the totalitarian interpretation, he vindicated Fichte as a cultural nationalist of resistance. He thought that the democratic nation must rest on the independence of each individual and the pursuit of freedom and peace; moreover, he believed that postwar Japan should become an ethical nation with high cultural ideals. Though he was critical of Marxism, which had been very influential in postwar Japan, he emphasized the importance of social rights and the justice of the people. In this sense, he was a social democrat.

It is widely recognized that his thought exerted much influence on the Fundamental Law of Education (教育基本法) established in 1947. I cite its essence here.

> Having established the Constitution of Japan, we have shown our resolution to contribute to the peace of the world and welfare of humanity by building a democratic and cultural state. The realization of this ideal shall depend on the power of education. We shall esteem individual dignity and endeavor to bring up people who love truth and peace, while education which aims at the creation of culture general and rich in individuality shall be spread far and wide … Education shall aim at the full development of personality, striving for the rearing of the people, sound in mind and body, who shall love truth and justice, esteem individual value, respect labor and have a deep sense of responsibility, and be imbued with the independent sprit, as builders of the peaceful state and society.

In my view, this educational idea is a perfectionist one based upon *virtue ethics* rather than Kantian ethics, though Nanbara was never an Aristotelian nor Thomist but rather a Kantian-Fichtean Christian. He believed that the development of the *democratic mind* could not be separated from *democratic education* and the *cultivation of humanity*. In sum, he thought that democracy presupposes the *democratic understanding of Self, Others, and Public World*. As I described in Chapter 3, Nanbara maintained that Japan should play an independent role for world peace and uphold the peace treaty with all belligerent nations, including China, India, the Soviet Union, etc. Therefore, his public philosophy presupposed both the *national and international Self*.

Nanbara's public philosophy remained, however, blind to *minority people* such as Koreans in Japan, who lost their national identity in the postwar period. *The national democratic understanding of Self and Others was not enough in this sense.* I have also pointed out his lack of thinking about the dimension and role of *civil society*, which cannot be identified with national political society. Indeed, as the first president of the University of Tokyo in postwar Japan, Nanbara's philosophy has an elitist limitation. Therefore, the influence of his democratic thought waned after his retirement.

On the other hand, the influence of Maruyama's democratic thinking on young people continued until the 1970s. He emphasized the importance of the connection of *the liberal-individualistic mind with the democratic mind* to overcome the system of irresponsibility prevailing in Japan. As was shown in Chapter 3, I highly appreciate Maruyama in several respects. His positive legacy must be taken up; especially because its heritage has been increasingly ignored and is even attacked by unsound nationalists now in Japan. For all that, I cannot but point out that his democratic thought has some limitations; i.e., the neglect of Asian people, including minorities in Japan, which began with the ideas of Yukichi Fukuzawa (described above). As a matter of fact, Maruyama seems to have overestimated Fukuzawa's enlightenment thought. What I miss in Maruyama as a great public philosopher in post-WWII Japan is the idea of *trans-national civil society*.

Transition to Part II

With the close of the Cold War era, the world entered the so-called "unstable age of globalization." Economic globalism seems to become more and more dominant all over the world, yet, on the other hand, anachronistic nationalism or ethnocentrism has begun to revive, as seen in the new notorious textbook on Japanese history. In this situation, the serious problem lies within the postwar Japanese government, which made it a rule to follow the international policies of the United States of America uncritically. Japanese intellectuals, too, are not without their faults, as they have focused on the modernization of the individual as a nation and have not attached much importance to the problems of overcoming the history of modern Japan in Asia. This is why Japan, unlike Germany, has not yet acquired the trust of Asian countries. To overcome such situations, we should co-memorize the different processes of modernizations and acknowledge our common future.

As for the future of democracy, I think we should develop the *trans-national democracy wherein the civil society rather than the government plays a great role, so as to cooperate with one another and deal with global issues* such as world peace, human rights, environmental problems, economic development, education, and so on. In this regard, I strongly support the *Preamble to the Japanese Constitution*, which declares the contributions of Japanese people to the world (as I mentioned in Chapter 1 and 3). I am convinced that it is just on the basis of the Japanese Constitution that Japan can contribute to developing the trans-national democracy or to what Australian political theorist John Keane (1949-) calls "Cosmocracy," which "stands on the spectrum between the so-called 'Westphalian' model of competing sovereign states and a single, unitary system of world government" and means "a conglomeration of interlocking and overlapping sub-state, state and supra-state institutions and multi-dimensional processes that interact, and have political and social effects, on a global scale."[10]

This task leads us to the next theme of civil society.

Part II

4.2 Developments of Ideas on Civil Society in Japan and Germany

In this part, I will discuss the developments of *ideas of civil society* not only in Japan but also in *Germany*. The reason why I discuss both countries is that modern Japanese history and German history have several similarities concerning the following points.

First, both countries started building their versions of the modern nation-state during a very close period; namely, 1868 in Japan and 1871 in Germany. Second, Japan established the Meiji Constitution in 1889 after the model of the Prussian Constitution. Third, many Japanese scholars studied in Germany and imported numerous German philosophies and social theories until WWII. Fourth, Japan allied with Nazi Germany in WWII and was defeated. Fifth, as defeated nations, Japan and Germany thus had to start their own postwar histories and were fated to overcome their pasts. Lastly, however, there is a big difference between them now with regard to their relation to neighboring countries.

Based upon these concerns, I will now discuss the historical development of ideas on Civil Society in Japan and Germany.

4.2.1 Developments of Ideas on Civil Society in Prewar Japan and Germany

Although there are some scholars who trace back the concept of civil society to *koinonia politike* (political community) in Aristotle or to *societas civilis* in Cicero, I conclude that it was not until in the middle of the 18th century that the term civil society came into use with an original meaning as distinct from political community. More exactly, it was *Adam Ferguson* (1723-1816) in Scotland who expanded this term into a normative key concept of a commerce society free from corruption.

10 See Keane [2003] p. 98.

In his book entitled *An Essay on the History of Civil Society*, published in 1767, Ferguson attached much importance to the virtues of citizens in order for civil society that was developed by private property, along with division of labors and trades, to avoid becoming corrupt. In this regard, Ferguson's view of civil society is *not only historical but also ethical*. Indeed, his view of civil society that was advanced in terms of *civic virtue* in the rising market society has maintained its actuality; especially in developing countries that have been suffering terrible corruptions (Ferguson [1995/1767]). Ferguson did not, however, distinguish civil society from the state.

Historically speaking, however, it is a great German philosopher, Georg Wilhelm *Hegel* (1770-1831), who altered Ferguson's concept and distinguished civil society under the name of *bürgerliche Gesellschaft* (bourgeois society) from the state.

In his famous book *Grundlinien der Philosophie des Rechts* published in 1821, Hegel characterized *bürgerliche Gesellschaft* (bourgeois society; hereafter bür G) as a society to be located between the family and the state. According to Hegel, bür G consists of two dimensions; i.e., the system of needs (*System der Bedürfnisse*) and institutions such as judiciary, *Polizei* for public welfare, and corporations. Accepting partly the mechanism of market economy as a new stage of modern society, but denying the harmonious development of it as Adam Smith believed, Hegel thought that the system of needs as an important component of bür G cannot but produce a disparity between the rich and the poor. He believed, therefore, that the other components of bür G should play a role to overcome such a disparity (Hegel [1970/1821]). In this regard, his view of bür G is not only descriptive but also normative.

Hegel thought, however, that it is not these institutions in the bür G but the ethical, constitutional, and monarchal state modeled on that of Prussia that realizes public welfare. He attached much importance to the role of government officials, who he considered fair and disinterested, in order to overcome the disparity and to realize public welfare (ibid.). In this regard, I would say that Hegel was a "forerunner of the theory of the modern welfare state."

While Marx attacked Hegel's idea of the state as an illusion, the Hegelian legacy was taken over by *Lorenz von Stein* (1815-1890): an eminent scholar on the constitutional state and public administration. Influenced both by Hegel and the socialist movement in France of those days, Stein understood the concept of society in a negative way as a field full of conflicts and struggles. On the other hand, he understood the constitutional state in a positive way as an ethical institution to overcome such conflicts and struggle. The reason why I talk about Stein here is that he influenced Japanese political heavyweights who carried national recognition, such as Itō Hirobumi (伊藤博文 1841-1909), as well as the organization of the Faculty of Law at the Imperial University of Tokyo in the Meiji period.[11]

In my view, the German idea of the welfare state called *Sozialstaat* (social state) could be derived from Hegel and Stein. However, I must point out that Stein's negative view of society stood backward in comparison with Hegel's view of civil society, which was described not only in a negative way but also a positive way, as I mentioned.

This tradition was taken over in the late 19th century by the *German Historical School* of Economics, which was interested in solving social problems not by socialist revolution but by governmental social policies.[12] This school was called *Kathedersozialismus* (professional socialism) and was represented by scholars such as A. Wagner (1835-1917) as a right-wing theorist, G. Schmoller (1838-1917) as a centrist, and L. Brentano (1844-1931) as a left-wing theorist. It should not be forgotten that economics in Japan began with the reception of the German Historical School. *Japanese Verein für Socialpolitik* (the Japanese Association for Social Policy), modeled after *German Verein für Socialpolitik* (the German Association for Social Policy), was founded in 1897.

From the viewpoint of the state/society distinction, I mentioned in Part 1 *Fukuda Tokuzō*: a promoter of Taishō Democracy, who, together with Yoshino Sakuzo, radically transformed Lorenz von Stein's idea. Fukuda had once studied in München under the guidance of L. Brentano, and, in his forgotten but still important book *Social Policy and Class Struggle* (published in 1922), he inverted the concept and relationship of society and state advanced by Stein. On the one hand, he regarded society as the field of social movement entailing the right of each person to exist according to the minimum standards of living: an idea that he borrowed from Anton Menger (a famous jurist in Austria, 1841-1906). On the other hand, he regarded the state as an institution that meets the demands of such a social movement and tries to realize social welfare (Fukuda [2015/1922]).

Although Fukuda did not use the term *civil society*, we can see him as a forerunner of civil society theorists; especially because he called his social theory 'democratic science.' Indeed, the time in which he actively worked is called Taishō Democracy.

As I described above, however, Fukuda's democratic ideas, as well as those of his more famous comrade Yoshino, were frustrated in the 1930s, during which time Japan made a mad dash for invasion into China. Mirroring Nazi Germany, democracy was changed into a kind of fascism in which liberal interpretation of the Meiji Constitution was suppressed and the emperor's despotism became more

---

11 For Stein's influence on Japanese statesmen and scholars, see Takii [1998].

12 For the German Historical School, see Shionoya [2001].

and more dominant. In this mobilization of the whole country, civil society had to be *absorbed into the political system of imperial state*.

As for Marxism in the Japan of those days, there were several eminent theorists such as *Kawakami Hajime* (河上肇 1879-1946), who argued with Fukuda Tokuzo and exerted much influence on Japanese leftist scholars and social movements. He did not, however, advance any theory of civil society; partly because Marx himself had described bür G (bourgeois society) negatively as the very selfish society of the bourgeoisie. Indeed, it was not in postwar Japan that the idea of civil society began to be used in a positive way by Neo-Marxian theorists.

4.2.2 Transformations of the Idea of Civil Society in Postwar Japan and Germany

After the Second World War, the new constitution was promulgated in 1947 and declared that sovereign power lies with the Japanese people. The status of emperor was also downgraded to a symbol of the state.

Articles 11 to 29 of the Japanese constitution guarantee human rights such as civil, political, and social rights. It deserves to be mentioned here that Article 25 states, "All people shall have the right to maintain the minimum standards of wholesome and cultured living." This means that the socio-economic right of the Japanese people was inspired not by the American idea of liberalism but by an idea of the *Weimar Constitution* established in 1919. It is widely acknowledged that the adoption of Article 25 was advocated by Morito Tatsuo (森戸辰男 1888-1984), who had just studied in the Weimar Republic.

Japanese society changed greatly during the 1960s, and the Tokyo Olympic Games were held in 1964. Contrary to the prediction of orthodox Marxists that the capitalist system in Japan would be ruined soon, the Japanese economy continued to grow; partly thanks to the Keynesian idea of economics and partly thanks to the leading bureaucrats and ministries located in Kasumigaseki, such as MITI (the Ministry of International Trade and Industry). It almost became a myth to think that a socialist system like that of the Soviet Union and its satellite states surpassed the capitalist system. At the same time, the radical student movement against the Vietnam War, out-of-date mentalities of university professors, and so on, occurred from the end of 1960s to the beginning of 1970s in Japan, as well as in the former West Germany.

However, unlike the political situation in the former West Germany, in which the SPD (Social Democratic Party) came into power in the 1970s, the political system in Japan (the so-called 55 system) did not change. The conservative party, named the Liberal-Democratic Party, was in power until 1993, while the Socialist Party as the largest opposition party was captured until the 1980s by ideology that still regarded the socialist system as an ideal and therefore rejected social democracy such as that endorsed by the SPD.

It was in this situation that the *Neo-Marxian idea of civil society* (*Shimin shakai* 市民社会) became popular among scholars. *Uchida Yoshiaki* (内田義彦 1913-89), who was influenced not only by Marx but also by Adam Smith, had been stressing since the 1950s the significance of civil society, in which the law of one price as commutative justice dominates (Uchida [1953]). *Hirata Kiyoaki* (平田清明 1922-95), on the other hand, stressed that socialism without civil society based on the property rights of individuals (*Einzelne*) would be barbaric (Hirata [1969]). Both scholars had in common the view that civil society was a "necessary precondition of socialism," and they believed that this would be actualized in the future. Although admired among some social theorists, this idea of civil society was not only ignored by conservatives but also harshly criticized by orthodox Marxists who believed in Marxism-Leninism and had considerable influence on both the Communist Party and the left wing of the Socialist Party.

What I miss in Uchida's, as well as Hirata's, idea of civil society is a theory of democracy. Since these men were not political theorists but rather economic theorists, they were not so interested in democratic theory. As a matter of fact, their thought was gradually forgotten, especially after the fall of the Berlin Wall, and even seems to have resulted in a bias against the concept of civil society among Japanese scholars and people.

Now, I would like to cast a glance over postwar Germany. As is well known, the miracle growth of the economy in postwar West Germany as led by the Adenauer regime, especially by Minister of Finance L. Erhard (1897-1977), was not based upon a Keynesian idea of economics but upon the so-called *Ordoliberalism* represented by W. Eucken (1891-1950), W. Röpke (1899-1966), and others. Although Ordoliberals emphasized the significance of social market economy (Müller-Armack) or talked about "Civitas Humana" (Röpke), the phrase "civil society" seems not to have been used by them.[13]

In the scholarly world, too, it was not until the publication of the epoch-making book *Strukturwandel der Öffentlichkeit* (The Structural Transformation of the Public Sphere), written by J. Habermas (1929-) in 1962, that the idea of bür Gesellschaft began to be spotlighted again in connection with Öffentlichkeit (the public sphere). Habermas as a young, new, left social theorist at that time advanced a study on the historical transformation of bürgeliche Öffentlichkeit (the bourgeois public sphere) in modern Europe; especially in England, France, and Germany since the 17th century (Habermas [1990/1962]). According to him, bürgerliche Öffentlichkeit, which had appeared among private citizens (Bürger) to criticize dynasties in the 17th and 18th centuries in Europe, declined gradually from

[13] For my own interpretation of Ordoliberalism, see Yamawaki [2001].

the 19th century due to what he later calls "colonization of lifeworld by the administrative power as well as by the monetary economy" (Habermas [1981]).

Apparently, his historical study intended to criticize the idea of social state put forward by Hegel, Stein, and the Historical School of Economics in terms of *Öffentlichkeit* (public sphere). Habermas held a radical democratic viewpoint, and this mode of thought did not attach much importance to the value of Öffentlichkeit, as Hegel's not always positive view of public opinion showed.

Due to space limitations, I do not enter into a comprehensive normative social theory based on the communicative action advanced by Habermas since the 1970s. Instead, I only point out here that he introduced a new important idea of *Zivilgesellschaft* (civil society) as distinct from bür G (bourgeois society) in the second edition of his aforementioned book, which was published in 1990 just after the collapse of the Berlin Wall.

Let me cite this paragraph about the topic:

> It also recalls the now current meaning of the term "civil society," which no longer includes a sphere of an economy regulated via labor, capital, and commodity markets and thus differs from the modern translation, common since Hegel and Marx, "*societas civilis*" as "bourgeois society" ("*bürgerliche Gesellschaft*"). Unfortunately, a search for clear definitions in the relevant publication is in vain. However, this much is apparent: the institutional core of "civil society" is constituted by voluntary unions outside the realm of the state and the economy and ranging (to give some examples in no particular order) from churches, cultural associations, and academies to independent media, sport and leisure clubs, debating societies, groups of concerned citizens, and grass-roots petitioning drives all the way to occupational associations, political parties, labor unions, and "alternative institutions."
>
> (J. Habermas [1990/1962], p.46, also in Calhoun [1992] pp.453-454)

In this way, Habermas distinguished civil society, which can be identified almost with the public sphere of citizens, from bür G, which includes the market economy. This idea is not always, however, accepted by scholars.

In the English-speaking world, for example, *Michael Walzer* (1935-), who I have already described in the second chapter as one of the communitarians of the US, defines civil society as "the space of uncoerced human association and also the set of relational networks – formed for the sake of family, faith, interest, and ideology – that fill this space" (Walzer [1995] p.7).

In the German-speaking world, *Rulf Dahrendorf* (1929-2009), who is regarded as a radical and liberal theorist in Germany, advocated a different concept of Burgergesellschaft, which has the following characteristics.

> 1) Diversity of its elements. For example, only one state church has nothing to do with civil society, but several churches independent of the state belong to civil society. 2) The autonomy of many organizations and institutions, including, above all, the independence

of the power center. Institutions financed by the state such as universities and small and middle enterprises are components of civil society. 3) The virtues of members against authoritative and totalitarian domination, etc. (Dahrendorf [1992] pp. 67-73, translated by me).

Thus, the German translation and definition of civil society are *not univocal* at present. In view of such a situation, in the subsequent chapters I will summarize current issues over civil society against the background of new international, as well as domestic, social situations. I will then put forward my own view of civil society based on a new public philosophy in which I have been engaged since the late 1990s.

4.2.3 Current Issues over Civil Society and My Own Stance

Hirata Kiyoaki's Neo-Marxian belief that socialism without civil society is barbaric and cannot endure was realized by the collapse of the socialist system in the Soviet Union and Eastern Europe. The non-governmental organizations in East European countries such as in Poland, Czechoslovakia, East Germany, etc., played very important roles in breaking down the authoritarian socialist regimes, and, since then, such organizations have gradually begun to be construed as civil society. At the same time, the public role of NGOs or INGOs began to be widely recognized around the world, while the concept of governance instead of government likewise came into being.

In Japan, too, a new wave of volunteerism occurred; especially on the occasion of the *Kobe (Great Hanshin-Awaji) earthquake* in January 1995. A new law was enacted to make it easier for citizens to organize nonprofit organizations (NPOs) in 1998. Nowadays, there are about 40,000 NPOs in Japan. Many private corporations also began to show interest in corporate social responsibility (CSR), which refers to the contribution of private corporations to environmental preservation and other issues. More than 50 Japanese corporations entered into global contact with the UN, which means that the corporations keep to ten principles regarding human rights, labor, environment, and prevention of corruption, decided by the UN.

In this way, not only the government but also NPOs (=NGOs) and even private companies have become actors that pursue public values. In parallel with these transformations, the concept of civil society has seemingly begun to be renewed and to be widely used in a sense other than that which Uchida and Hirata had once conceived. While these theorists conceived civil society as the pre-stage of socialism, civil society in contemporary Japan refers to the area in which non-governmental organizations and individual citizens publicly act.

Still, there remain important issues that are not easily solved. I will summarize them here and then present my own views on these topics.

1. The first and perhaps most polemic issue is whether the market economy belongs to civil society or not. As mentioned, Habermas, who identified civil society (*Zivilgesellschaft*) with the public sphere, excludes the market economy from civil society. On the other hand, though each has his own concept, Walzer and Dahrendorf, both seem to include the market economy in civil society.
   My own view on this issue is that *the concept of civil society is wider than that of public world, and, therefore, it may include the market economy.* In this regard, I differ from Habermas' idealistic view of civil society, although I have learned much from his thought on the public sphere (or public world) and the "colonization of lifeworld by the administrative power as well as the monetary economy." Therefore, my stance may be closer to Walzer's and Dahrendorf's more realistic view, and even I can revaluate Hegel's classical idea of bür G. This includes both market economy, which is full of conflicts, and institutions such as corporations, which try to solve conflicts caused by market economy; however, I reject Hegel's Euro-centric view of world history, as well as his denial of cosmopolitanism.
2. With this in mind, I have to take up the next issue about the *relationship between the actors of civil society and the public world.* To be sure, both overlap with each other, but they are not always the same. Private companies as important actors of market economy cannot be said to be important actors of the public world so far as their main aim is profit-seeking. Private companies can take part in the public world only through CSR (Corporate Social Responsibility). As for NGOs and NPOs in a broad sense, it must be said that their legitimacy is based on their accountability for their public action. However, there are many NPOs in Japan that do not put this accountability into practice. It cannot be said, therefore, that all NPOs play this role in the public world, which can only operate successfully according to *public values.*
   In my view, *the public world is more normative than civil society.* The former (=public world) has much to do with public values such as human rights, peace, welfare, etc., as well as negative values such as war, poverty, political suppression, etc. Its actors can be called "the public (公衆)" as "a set of people who share a common interest and activity with civic virtues." On the other hand, the latter (=civil society) has something to do with such public values but it also contains 'conflicts of interests' among institutions and citizens.
3. From this viewpoint, I cannot but take up the issue of *methodology for discussing civil society.* I am of the opinion that the *three-dimensional method of learning* that was introduced in Chapter 2 must be applied here, as below.
   The first component consists of empirical research, which analyzes and describes historical processes and the present realities of civil society. This ap-

proach is concerned with the question of *what we must know*. Indeed, I adopted this approach in part during this chapter.

The second component consists of normative visions, which discuss the topic of what kind of civil society is most desirable. This approach is concerned with the question of *what we should do*. I will take up this vision in the next section.

The third component consists of public policies, which pursue the feasibility of realizing public values such as peace, welfare, and human rights, and eliminating negative values such as poverty, political suppression, crimes, war, terrorism, etc., in civil societies. This approach is concerned with the question of *what we can do and how we can do so*. I will also take up this problem in the next section.

4.3 Toward Trans-national Civil Society on the Basis of *Glocal Ontology and Trans-national Public Ethics*

Based upon this formulation, I believe that it is a desideratum for the Japanese people and intellectuals to construct the *transnational democratic public world and civil society*, together with other Asian countries, as a Japanese *glocal* task.

To put forward this task, the *role of civil society* in distinction from the government has to become more and more important. Civil society in Japan, however, remains weak when compared to Western countries, and this particularly the case when compared to Germany as a nation likewise defeated in WWII. As a matter of fact, while German civil society made a great contribution to the reconciliation of the countries in Europe, civil society in Japan lagged behind in reconciling with other Asian countries.

Facing these circumstances and faults, it is indispensable for Asian people to conceive of the *trans-national public world and civil society*, which go beyond the nation-state and enable trans-national cooperation to work; especially in view of the contemporary unstable age of globalization. We first need the *multi-dimensional, responsive, dialogical, and becoming Self,* which I advocated in the previous chapters as a *glocal ontology* that opposes the one-dimensional, nationalistic, imperialistic, irresponsible, monological, and static Self. Second, we need a *trans-national public ethics* that tries to promote *trans-national public values* such as world peace, human rights, wellbeing, the natural environment, etc., and to overcome past historical errors and usher in our common futures. I hope the *trans-national civil society empowered by this glocal ontology and public ethics* will play a very important role in enabling the respective governments to realize more peaceful and just societies.

5 A New Orientation of Philosophy and Ethics after March 11, 2011

The great disaster of March 11, 2011, shocked not only the Japanese people but also people all over the world. In my view, the "earthquake and tsunami" that occurred on this day may be called "natural disasters," but the "accident of the nuclear power plants in Fukushima" that was caused by the earthquake and Tsunami was evidently a "human-made disaster." Indeed, the impact of the Fukushima accident was so great that the governments of other countries were forced into reconsidering their energy policies. As a matter of fact, the German government decided on the permanent abolishment of nuclear power by 2022 on the basis of the proposal of the *Ethics Commission* founded by Chancellor Merkel shortly after the Fukushima accident. In other countries, too, energy politics is becoming more and more important. In this sense, the disaster on March 11, 2011, can be called a serious *glocal* event.

Starting from this concern, the present chapter will consider the new orientation of philosophy and ethics after March 11, 2011. To pursue this theme, I think it indispensable to reconstruct the *history of nuclear power* from the end of the 1930s to the present as "an unfinished grand narrative." Before reconstructing it, however, and in order for us to make the philosophical importance of *nuclear energy* widely known, it is necessary to point out that there is an undeniable desideratum in the "theory of modernity" as a contemporary public philosophy in Western countries.

5.1 A Desideratum on the Theory of Modernity as Contemporary Public Philosophy

In my view, the philosophical issue of modernity in Western countries since the 1980s began with a controversial book, *The Postmodern Condition*, written by the French philosopher Jean-François Lyotard in 1979.

Lyotard formulated that "modernity" can be characterized by the pursuit of progress, while "post-modernity" can be expressed as incredulity towards the various 'grand narratives' of progress such as the progress of history, the knowability of everything by science, and the possibility of absolute freedom. According to Lyotard, the people of today have ceased to believe that narratives of this kind are adequate for representing our world and, instead, have become alert to difference, diversity, and the incompatibility of our aspirations, beliefs, and desires. From such a viewpoint, Lyotard developed a postmodern theory of justice in his later work (Lyotard [1979]). He believed that the universality of ethics had become obsolete and that public values such as justice and injustice in the postmodern era can be discussed only within language games. Ethical and just behavior is now evaluated on the basis of whether or not one pays attention to unjust things in their particular various language games (Lyotard [1983]).

This "postmodern theory" of Lyotard seems, however, to have become obsolete in view of the real historical events that have occurred since the 1990s. The Gulf War, the Yugoslav Civil War, the Kosovo conflicts, the September 11 terror attacks, and the March 11 disaster showed that we *do* need a grand theory, not only about history but also about culture and nature, without falling into the progressivism that Lyotard criticized. His view of ethics within language games is too narrow to deal with wide-ranging ethical issues in this situation. That is why I regard Lyotard's theory as unconvincing and out-of-date.

On the other hand, the German public philosopher J. Habermas (who I discussed in the previous chapters) has defended, since the beginning of the 1980s, the modern enlightenment thought against postmodernism and has instead rehabilitated the notion of *modernity as an unfinished project* (Habermas [1981/1980]). He believes that the project of modernity must be reconstructed by the "communicative actions of public citizens" upon the basis of "discourse ethics." With this project, he set out to foster the revitalization of "participatory democracy and public space" that administrative power and monetary economy have been obstructing. Since then, he has been developing this defense of modernity into a grand narrative of New Europe based upon the "European Constitution," which will overcome the limits of modern nation-states and anticipate the World Federation in the future. In this regard, he tries to renew Kant's idea of the world citizen in the 21st century (Habermas [1981], [1991], [2011]).

Indeed, this bold intention of Habermas as a "trans-national" public philosopher deserves to be appreciated. To be sure, it will continue to be a great source for the conception of the democratic world order. Still, as I have criticized in Chapter 2, Habermas' thinking remains too idealistic and too Eurocentric to take the diversity of world cultures into account. His discourse ethics in this sense is too idealistic to realize among various cultures. As a matter of fact, the international situation at present remains far from Habermas' dream.

In distinction from Habermas, the Canadian public philosopher Charles Taylor and his research group for trans-cultural studies advocated, instead of speaking of "modernity in the singular," speaking of *multiple modernities* that take the diversity of cultures into account. This term itself seems to be derived from Israeli sociologist S.N. Eisenstadt,[1] but Taylor and his research group attempt to formulate the concept of multiple modernities in a more intensive way. According to them, it means "the picture of a plurality of human cultures, each of which has a language and a set of practices which define specific understandings of personhood, social relations, states of mind/soul, goods and bads, virtues and vices, and the like." Therefore, where there exists an unsituated, disengaged subject who has an overview of everything and for whom being situated produces biases, this situation needs to be overcome. This "view from nowhere" forms a presupposition not only for the natural sciences but for any type of research. The modern nation-state relies on the instrumentalities of objective research (economic statistics, maps, censuses) that institutionalize the "view from nowhere" as a fundamental presupposition of the international order.[2]

Thus, instead of research that holds an a-cultural viewpoint on society and culture, Taylor considers that there are now *different social imaginaries* of research developing. Research and the multiple ethics that might support it could be topics of discussion and debate among scholars and cultural practitioners from other societies and traditions of inquiry (Taylor [2004]). I very much appreciate this notion of multiple modernities proposed by Taylor as a contemporary great public philosopher and his research group; especially because it stands very close to the idea of *glocal* public philosophy conceived in this book, which rejects the "view from nowhere" and instead adopts the *view from locally situated Self, Others, and Public World*. Indeed, it will continue to be an important source of our thinking.

Still, I have to say that there is a desideratum even in Taylor's excellent concept of multiple modernities. I mean by a "desideratum" the *public philosophy on nature, technology, and science* that definitely characterized the traits of modernity. It seems to me curious that the researchers exclude the grand narrative of the *modern progress of technology and science* that caused huge disasters such as atom bombing and threats to the survival of humankind. This theme should become a very serious public issue in multiple modernities as a great narrative.

---

[1] See Eisenstatd [2002].

[2] For this project attempted by Taylor and Lee, see the University of Pennsylvania's Center for Transcultural Studies: http://www.sas.upenn.edu/transcult/promad.html.

5.2 The History of *Nuclear Energy as an Unfinished Grand Narrative* in the Modern Era

Now that I have expressed my dissatisfactions with these influential theories on modernity in contemporary Western public philosophy, I will reconstruct the history of *nuclear power* as an unfinished grand narrative in the modern era.

5.2.1 From Discovery of Nuclear Energy to the Manhattan Project

In my view, the history of nuclear power as a grand narrative began with the Manhattan Project.[3] Learning that German physical chemists Otto Hahn and Fritz Strassmann had discovered nuclear-fission in Berlin 1938 and that the famous physicist Lise Meitner had proved it in Scandinavia, prominent physicists such as Leo Szilard and Eugene Wigner drafted the so-called Einstein-Szilard letter, which warned of the potential development of "extremely powerful bombs of a new type." They urged President Franklin D. Roosevelt to establish a program to study the potential military use of nuclear fission, and, by 1942, the project was code-named Manhattan. In 1943, a laboratory to construct the bomb was established and staffed by scientists headed by J. Robert Oppenheimer. By its end, the project had cost some 2 billion dollars and required 125,000 people. It was in this project that plutonium was artificially produced by neutron irradiation of uranium-238. The success of this project resulted in the atom bombings using uranium-235 in Hiroshima and plutonium-239 in Nagasaki.

After WWII, Theodor Adorno as a representative of Critical Theory discussed the dialectic of enlightenment and talked about the possibility or impossibility of poetry and philosophy after *Auschwitz* (Adorno [1983/1955] pp. 17-34.). He seems, however, not to have talked about the seriousness of *Hiroshima and Nagasaki* so much. In my view, apart from Bertrand Russell (who served as the first president of the international *Pugwash Conferences* on nuclear weapons and world security, and who led the worldwide campaign for nuclear disarmament), the exceptional European philosopher who took the atom bombing in Hiroshima and Nagasaki seriously was Günther Anders, who was the first husband of Hannah Arendt. Indeed, he visited Hiroshima and Nagasaki in 1958 and wrote many articles on the threat of nuclear power.[4]

As a matter of fact, the history of world politics after WWII can be seen as the history of the arms race. Even the slogan *Atoms for Peace*, which was the title of a speech made by US President Dwight Eisenhower to the UN General Assembly on December 8, 1953, sounded like a kind of rhetorical maneuver for the US's new alliances; including Japan. About three months after this speech, on March 1, 1954,

---

3 On the history of the nuclear bomb, see Rose [2012/1986].

4 See Anders [1995].

a Japanese fishing boat known as the fifth Fukuryu Maru was exposed to a fall of radioactive ash caused by the US's thermonuclear test at *Bikini Atoll*, although the boat was away from the restricted area. Regrettably, a chief radio operator died half a year later. Following this occasion, anti-nuclear movements in Japan arose strongly among citizens and leftist parties, but they were not so successful when faced with the arms race in which the US, USSR, France, England, China, and India were engaged.

The famous German sociologist Ulrich Beck (1944-2015), who was the author of *Risk Society* (Beck [1986]), said recently in an interview with a Japanese journalist that he could not understand why Japan has been promoting the nuclear plants policy when it is the only country that has endured atomic bombings in Hiroshima and Nagasaki.[5] I think his question is just and sensible, and, as a Japanese scholar, I therefore feel obliged to provide an answer.

5.2.2 The Illusion of Nuclear Power Plants as Atoms for Peace

With a sidelong and even scornful glance at anti-nuclear movements after the fifth Fukuryu Maru accident, the Japanese conservative political elite such as Nakasone Yasuhiro and Shōriki Matsutaro decided to develop nuclear power as a new energy source under the *Atoms for Peace Program*. They introduced and passed some bills related to nuclear power, while one of the biggest newspapers in Japan (*Yomiuri*) strongly supported the *Atoms for Peace Program* and organized a grand exhibition to promote it successfully. They regarded *Atoms for Peace* as an industrial revolution and an alternative to oil. In this way, the first nuclear electric power plant at *Tōkai* village began to operate in 1966, and another nuclear power plant at *Tsuruga* city succeeded in offering electric power for the Osaka Expo in 1970.[6]

The so-called oil shock in the 1970s made many Japanese people believe that nuclear power was a genuine alternative to oil. Prime Minister Kakuei Tanaka passed three bills supporting it as a source of electricity and decided to offer official subsidies for cities, towns, or villages that accepted nuclear power plants. He also forged a connection with France in order to introduce the technology for recycling plutonium. In spite of the major accident at *Three Mile Island* on March 28, 1979, and at *Chernobyl* on April 26, 1986, public opinion in Japan has been more and more supportive of the promotion of nuclear power. This tendency of public opinion was, however, more or less manipulated by the Japanese government, large electric companies, and uncritical opportunist scholars, who are now called members of the "nuclear power village." Without any careful examination and even with a policy of covering up of repeated critical accidents, they created a "myth of the safety of the nuclear power plant" as a clean source of energy that

5 This interview with Beck appeared in *Asahi Newspaper* in Japanese on May 13, 2011.

6 On the history of the nuclear plant in Japan, I owe much to an excellent book by Yoshioka [2011].

can overcome the crisis of global warming. The propaganda of nuclear power as a clean energy source thus deadened people's power of reasoning.

The enormous accident in Fukushima shows clearly that nuclear technology, which transforms uranium as a native element of nature into plutonium as an almost artificial product, really does harm to human beings. It produces "high-level radioactive waste" and therefore needs "permanent underground waste repositories" that we have not yet found. In my view, such negative aspects force us into questioning the idea of *Atoms for Peace* that Eisenhower advocated in 1953 and that has been widely accepted among developing countries.

Therefore, it would be illusionary to believe in *Atoms for Peace*, which derives from Eisenhower's speech. What I mean by this is that nuclear power entails intrinsic danger and public harm. Its intrinsic danger is the *radiation* and its intrinsic public harm comes in the form of *nuclear waste*.

As a matter of fact, the meltdown of a nuclear reactor in the accident at Fukushima shows the extent and irreparability of the danger posed by nuclear power. No one can declare yet whether the Japanese government and Tokyo Electric Power Company (TEPCO) regained control of this accident. There seems to be no consensus among scientists regarding the degree of danger that the radioactive materials such as cesium or fluorine emitted from the reactors pose to the people in Fukushima. Some people in other countries might say that this danger is not applicable to the countries in which earthquakes or tsunamis do not occur. In my view, however, they are wrong, because there are other risks such as terrorism or airplane accidents. Furthermore, as the most important issue, the problem of "high-level radioactive waste" remains unsettled.

The reason why I consider the problem of radioactive waste a public bad lies in the fact that "future generations" must pay for our benefit. As we use nuclear power more and more, the amount of radioactive waste will become larger and larger. This means that we expose future generations to a more unpleasant and risky society. In this regard, there is *certain continuity* between Hiroshima/Nagasaki and Fukushima, as the artificial product of *plutonium* shows.

5.3 Positive and Negative Effects of Bacon's Dream

Now, I would like to evaluate the modern history of technology in general so that we will be able to conceive public eco-philosophy in the 21st century.

When we trace the history of the philosophy of science and technology, we must reconsider Francis Bacon's idea of the progress of history, which was advanced about 500 years ago and exerted a great influence on modern enlightenment thinkers. Bacon thought, namely, that knowledge is embodied in the form of new technological inventions and mechanical discoveries that can drive history for the benefit of humankind, as shown by three inventions of his days; i.e. the compass, the printing press, and gunpowder. Believing in the progress of history by means of technological powers that dominate nature, he denied the scholastic teleological view of nature and advocated the human-centric use of nature instead. According to him, nature should be dominated for the sake of our benefit and happiness (Bacon [1963/1605]).

Though he did not live to see the triumph of his program, his idea was taken over by French encyclopedists such as Jean d'Alembert and Denis Diderot, who hailed Bacon as a founding father of the modern era and emblazoned his name on the front page of the Encyclopedia. And it was Condorcet that developed the idea of the continuous progress of humankind to an ultimate perfection in his famous *Sketch for a Historical Picture of the Progress of the Human Mind* (Condorcet [2009/1795]). Thus, Bacon's idea seems to have triumphed at the end of the 18th century.

One question arises now. Has this idea really triumphed? My answer is both Yes and No. My affirmative answer lies in the undeniable fact that we can enjoy many benefits of technology and science today thanks to such progress. It would be silly and self-contradictory to deny this fact. Just imagine our life without electricity, medicines, trains, cars, or airplanes – we cannot but say these are great achievements of Bacon's program. On the other hand, my negative answer relates closely to the progress of military armament. Let us recall the history of the 20th century. Through the experiences of two World Wars, we recognized that the progress of military technology caused genocide. Even the progress of science could produce a dangerous result, as the history of nuclear power described above shows. After WWII, the progress of military technology and scientific experiments for military use did not cease; rather, it produced the so-called ABC (atomic, biological, and chemical) weapons. In my view, this ironical result of technological progress had begun with Bacon already when he did not predict any risks of gunpowder as the great invention of his days.

The disaster caused by the great earthquake in Japan on March 11, 2011, urges us to rethink the relationship between human beings and nature. We have to rethink this disaster in two aspects.

First, the *tsunami* caused by the earthquake took more than 20,000 human lives and made us recognize the horrible aspects of nature. We cannot prevent earthquakes or tsunamis from happening, and, therefore, we have to say that complete domination over nature will always be impossible. What we can do in this regard is, at best, to prepare for unexpected natural disasters by means of reinforcing earthquake-proof structures, building breakwaters higher than 15 meters on the coast, or, instead, providing new training for seeking refuge in some places. In any case, we should be more cautious about disasters caused by nature and should abandon excessive trust in technology for the domination of nature. Or, rather, we must realize that we are not able to dominate nature as we would want. We should think of the human being not as the subject that stands outside nature (as Bacon and Descartes thought) but as belonging to nature in a particular manner. In other words, the human being could harmonize with non-human nature as well as do harm to non-human nature.

Second, the disaster in Fukushima has quite different traits to the tsunami, although it was caused by an earthquake and a tsunami. I mean by this that it was not a natural disaster but a human-made disaster. It is not enough for us to say that this disaster was due to the destruction of electric power sources in nuclear power. We have to say that this disaster occurred due to our "underestimation of the risk of the nuclear power plant." The harmful effect of radioactivity is so widespread and so uncertain that we cannot calculate the amount of damage to the economy and human body at present and in the future. The claim that nuclear power is safe and clean has proved to be false. This enormous accident shows clearly that nuclear technology, which transforms uranium and plutonium as native elements in nature to contribute to human welfare, can do harm to human beings.

The negative effect of nuclear power is more extensive than this. As I pointed out above, it produces high-level radioactive waste and therefore requires permanent underground waste repositories. As Professor Takagi Jinzaburō (高木仁三郎 1938-2000), whose excellent philosophical message I will take up in the last section of this chapter, had warned us, it would be an illusion to think that we can recycle spent nuclear fuel. As a matter of fact, not only a fast-breeder reactor called *Monju* in Tsuruga city but also a nuclear fuel cycle plant in *Rokkasho* village in Aomori still do not function, although the Japanese government has been spending a substantial budget on them every year. When we use nuclear power more and more, the amount of waste will become larger and larger. This means that we expose future generations to a more unpleasant and risky society. We should regard such a situation as unethical and develop both a new eco-public philosophy and new public ethics.

5.4 Public Eco-philosophy after Bacon's Dream

I will now introduce some new public eco-philosophies both in Europe and in East Asia, following on from Bacon's dream.

5.4.1 Ecological Metaphysics and Ethics in Europe – Hans Jonas and Robert Spaemann

In my view, the most important work of public eco-philosophy for future generations in the contemporary world is *Hans Jonas'* (1903-93) *The Imperative of Responsibility*, published in 1979. It should be pointed out, however, that Jonas was not only a great ethical scholar but also a famous philosopher on life. Therefore, I introduce his quasi-Aristotelian view on life, which comprises both philosophy of organism and philosophy of mind.

Jonas' famous book *The Phenomenon of Life*, published in 1966, aimed to break through the anthropocentric confines of idealist and existentialist philosophy, as well as through the materialist confines of natural science (Jonas [1966]). In contrast to modern philosophy that denies the teleological understanding of nature and adopts the dualism of nature and human mind, Jonas regards the human being as a part of organic nature (as in Aristotle's view of *De anima*) and adheres to a teleological view of nature, which, however, takes the evolutionary worldview into account. According to him, not only human beings but also other animals and even plants possess minds (ibid. pp. 99ff). The first form of freedom that plants, animals, and human beings have in common is metabolism, and the second form of freedom consists of motility, perception, and emotion. The third form of freedom lies in the faculty of image-making that only the human being possesses. In this faculty, the human being can reflect on Self, Others, and World, imagine his or her mortality, despair of his or her life, and even commit suicide (ibid. pp. 135ff).

Emphasizing the continuity as well as discontinuity between plants, animals, and human beings in this way, and breaking away from his former professor Heidegger, who still represented the dualism of human beings and other animals and who did not show any interest in social ethics or Nomos (ibid. pp. 211ff), Jonas advocated his own ethics on the ontological basis of this philosophy of life. It is just in this perspective that Jonas published his *The Imperative of Responsibility* (Jonas [1979], [1984]). We can regard this ontology and ethics as a great public eco-philosophy that we should adopt for the 21st century, and which lacks the representative public philosophies of Rawls, the communitarians, Arendt, Habermas, Taylor, and others. I will take it up again in 5.5.2.

In this connection, I would like to mention a famous German philosopher, *Robert Spaemann* (1927-), as a new eco-philosopher and Catholic public ethicist who has been criticizing nuclear energy since the 1950s. According to him, it is not enough to rely on the discourse ethics that Habermas advocates for dealing with nature. Spaemann considers the human being a part of organic nature, and, like Jonas, stresses the responsibility for the future generations. While Jonas seldom referred to nuclear energy, however, Spaemann has been criticizing the nuclear energy that was discovered in 1938, developed and applied to nuclear weapons during World War II, and used as nuclear power under the name *Atoms for Peace* (Spaemann [2011] pp. 101ff). The main reason why he opposes nuclear power is that it produces nuclear waste that human beings cannot manage and places a very heavy burden on future generations. It is also highly irresponsible to operate any nuclear power plant without finding a permanent underground nuclear waste repository (ibid. pp. 13ff). With this eco-ethical viewpoint, Spaemann has been a philosophical champion of anti-nuclear power since the 1980s and has exercised great influence on the rather conservative intellectuals and Catholic Church in Germany.

In addition, Spaemann has been aiming at the integration of duty-based ethics as above, as well as the virtue ethics that relates closely to human flourishing and benevolence on the basis of Catholic tradition (Spaemann [1989]), while Jonas' ethics is strongly characterized by duty-based ethics. Therefore, against the view of Habermas, who regards Spaemann as a Neo-Aristotelian conservative (Habermas [1981] p. 463), I regard him as a pioneer of public eco-philosophy for the 21st century.

5.4.2 Other Remarkable Eco-philosophers in Japan and China – Imamichi Tomonobu (今道友信) and Tu Weiming (杜維明)

In parallel to these Western trends, there are a few advocates of public eco-philosophy in Japan. I confine myself here to mentioning a world-known philosopher, *Imamichi Tomonobu* (1925-2012).

What Imamichi advocated is *eco-ethica*, which encompasses our human habitat and represents an ethics for our contemporary world and its scientific and technological environment. Therefore, it could be called a *meta-technica* (Imamichi [2009]). According to Imamichi, our responsibility should be oriented not only toward other human beings (*ethica ad hominem*), as Tetsuro Watsuji (who I discussed in Chapter 3) had once conceived, but also toward nature and things (*ethica ad rem*). Therefore, not only traditional virtues such as courage, loyalty, humility, and responsibility, but also new virtues such as love of strangers (*philoxenia*), punctuality, cosmopolitanism, mastery of languages and equipment, mental diversion (*eutrapelia*), etc., must be learned by everyone. The self-regulation of technology and humans as a form of social ethics is also indispensable.

As for nuclear energy, Imamichi quotes not only the *myth of Prometheus* but also Izanami, who was *Shinto's* goddess and died because she had borne the god of fire; indeed, Izanami warned before the Fukushima disaster that this dangerous modern fire should not be used without two ethical principles of ensuring safety and peaceful purposes. He was of the opinion that researchers, business leaders, and workers involved with nuclear energy must take up a revolution in moral consciousness and in dialog with philosophers, and he proposed a major institution for putting into practice these safety issues and this new ethics (ibid. pp. 70-73). This proposal from a famous conservative philosopher with many acquaintances in the business community in Japan was almost ignored then, but the warning has now proved to be true.

What I miss in Imamichi's idea is political philosophy combining his eco-ethica with the real public world, which I will mention later in 5.5.2. On this note, it would be a great task to develop his eco-ethica in a more public-philosophical way.

On the other hand, the world-famous Chinese philosopher Tu Weiming (1940-) has been trying to revive *Neo-Confucianism* as an eco-philosophy for the 21st century. According to him, Neo-Confucianism does not separate the understanding of Self from that of community and cosmos, and it contains both relational ethics and cosmology. Therefore, it can offer an alternative to an a-cosmic public ethics in Western countries. Against the current non-ecological public philosophy, especially in the English-speaking world, he has stressed repeatedly that the legacy of *Neo-Confucian public philosophy* attaches much importance to ecological circumstances, as it integrates cosmology and ethics and can therefore modify the one-sided project of enlightenment in Western countries. He also emphasises the ethics of responsibility for the future (Tu [2006], [2011]).

Indeed, for Tu Weiming, the *Communal, Ecological, and Responsive Self* constitutes a cardinal ontological value. In this sense, he deserves to be called a *Neo-Confucian Eco-philosopher*. He does not, however, discuss actual problems such as nuclear energy and weapons, and he seems to avoid treating urgent problems such as human rights. It remains to be seen how he or his disciples will deal with these issues.

Apart from my requirements above, we can regard these elements as new beginnings of a public eco-philosophy in East Asia, which tries to replace the modernistic ideology of domination over nature and to link the philosophical understandings of nature, ethics, and technology with one another. This would surely *enrich and renew our understanding of Public World, Self, and Others*.

5.5 Toward a New Public Ethics after Fukushima

Now I would like to discuss public ethics after the nuclear disaster in Fukushima. Generally speaking, there is no public philosophy without public communication, communicative reason, and public values such as justice, peace, human rights, wellbeing, etc. Based upon this premise, I would like first to conceive the relatively new but very important concepts of *risk communication and human securities*, as well as *human development*, and, second, to integrate relatively old ethical concepts of *duty ethics, virtue ethics*, and ethics of positive as well as negative *values*, which I discussed at the end of Chapter 2.

5.5.1 Ethics of Risk Communication and Human Security and Development

I begin with the concept of *risk communication*, which I think is very important for people suffering from the *threat of radiation* after the nuclear plant accident. Although five years have passed since the Fukushima nuclear plant disaster, the issue of the effects of nuclear radiation on the human body remains highly significant.

As a matter of fact, there are some leading Japanese experts on the effects of nuclear radiation, as well as radiological health safety risk management advisers, who regard the situation of Fukushima as follows.

> Below that threshold [100 millisievert] we cannot prove a higher risk for cancer. That is the evidence from research in Hiroshima, Nagasaki and Chernobyl. The International Commission on Radiological Protection suggests a limit between 20 and 100 millisievert in a situation with a nuclear emergency. Which threshold you pick is a political decision. You must weigh the risks and benefits, because any evacuation will also have any risks. The Japanese government chose the most careful radiological approach. That made people more confused and insecure ... They are not scientists, they are not doctors, they are not radiation specialists. They do not know the international standards, which researchers worked on very hard. It makes me sad that people believe gossip, magazines and even Twitter.
>
> In a situation where people had no understanding of radioactivity at all, I wanted to be very clear. I have now changed my communications approach from black-and-white to gray scale ... With low radiation doses the people have to decide for themselves whether to stay or to leave. Nobody can make that decision for them. They have to weigh the risks and the benefits: Moving can mean a loss of jobs and having to change schools for the children. These factors cause stress ... Tepco and the Japanese government support people in the decisions ... We know from Chernobyl that the psychological consequences are enormous. Life expectancy of the evacuees dropped from 65 to 58 years – not because of cancer, but because of depression, alcoholism and suicide. Relocation is not easy, the stress is very big.[7]

In my view, however, this way of thinking is "strongly utilitarian as well as elitist" and makes the ordinary people in Fukushima more anxious and irritated because it lacks the concept of *risk communication*. According to the *National Research Council* (NRC), risk communication (RC) means "*an interactive process of exchange of information and opinion among individuals, groups, and institutions. It involves multiple messages about the nature of risk and other messages, not strictly*

[7] This is Professor Yamashita Shunichi's statement in his interview with *Spiegel* on August 19, 2011. See http://www.spiegel.de/international/world/studying-the-fukushima-aftermath-people-are-suffering-from-radiophobia-a-780810.html.

about risk, that express concerns, opinions, or reactions to risk messages or to legal or institutional arrangements for risk management." This definition includes discussions about risk types and levels and about methods for managing risks. Specifically, the process is defined by levels of involvement in decisions, actions, or policies aimed at managing or controlling health or environmental risks. Therefore, risk communication should be understood as "a *complex, multidisciplinary, multidimensional, and evolving process of increasing importance in protecting the public's health*."[8]

Regarding the communication of radiation exposure control or radioactive doses, it would be wrong to understand it as an act of "enlightenment from above," as many medical doctors tend to do. We should understand it as "a public communication between specialists and the ordinary people, each of whom are stakeholders of risk and interest." In this respect, risk communication requires not only special knowledge about radioactive medical sciences but also an "ethics for specialists" such as medical doctors and clinical nurses, who should treat those concerned as subjects with equal human rights. According to WHO, health is defined as "a state of complete physical, mental and social well-being and not merely the absence of disease or infirmity."

In my view, this ethics of wellbeing and social right has to be combined with the ethics of *human securities*, which was introduced by *the Commission on Human Security*. This commission was founded as the result of an initiative launched in September 2000 by the prime minister of Japan, the late Keizō Obuchi (小渕恵三). The former United Nations high commissioner for refugees, Sadako Ogata (緒方貞子) and the Nobel Prize-winning Amartya Sen (who I already mentioned in Chapter 2) were appointed as its co-chairs. The commission defines the aim of *human security*, which differs from *state security*, as being "to reduce, and where possible eliminate, the danger and fear which threatens human life" and "to reduce the risks of instability." The concept of *human security* is intended to focus our attention directly on "risks which can lead to more serious consequences," thereby improving the quality of development in a complementary manner. The most urgent task for the program of human security is to establish a system that can react rapidly and appropriately to life-threatening situations. Such situations include the spread of infectious diseases such as AIDS, malaria, SARS, avian flu and swine flu, and, now, the Fukushima disaster.[9]

As for the ethics of human securities in this sense, it is very important to realize that the utilitarian approach, which regards the greatest happiness of the greatest

---

[8] See the National Research Council [1989] and the U.S. Public Health Service [1995].

[9] For Human Securities, see the Commission on Human Security [2003]: http://reliefweb.int/sites/reliefweb.int/files/resources/91BAEEDBA50C6907C1256D19006A9353-chs-security-may03.pdf

number as justice, is not enough. Therefore, other approaches such as Rawls' *Theory of Justice*, which aims at guaranteeing human rights both as "political and social rights," and the communitarians' idea of "common good" and "solidarity" with suffering peoples are required, too.[10] In addition, the perspective of Mary Kaldor (1947-), who considers the primacy of human rights, legitimate political authority, the bottom-up approach, etc., as the principles of human security seems insightful.[11]

In my view, this idea corresponds to the 25th article of Japanese constitution, which states, "All people shall have the right to maintain the minimum standards of wholesome and cultured living. In all spheres of life, the State shall use its endeavors for the promotion and extension of social welfare and security, and of public health." In my view, this new concept of *human securities* can be regarded as a *trans-national positive value*, because the aim of *human security* is different from that of state security; namely, it seeks "to reduce, and where possible eliminate, the danger and fear which threatens human life" and "to reduce the risks of instability," which can be seen as *trans-national public negative values*.

At the same time, it would be necessary to restore the peoples and towns suffering in the wake of disaster. In this respect, I believe that Amartya Sen's idea of *human development* should be adopted. As is widely known, Sen regards *economic* development not as an "end" but as a "means" for *human* development and proposes that development should be considered a "process of expanding real freedoms." Examples of these real freedoms include political participation, access to basic education, and healthcare. For this reason, we must focus attention during the process of economic development on the elimination of major factors involved in the deprivation of freedoms. Among these factors are poverty, physical and mental stress, lack of economic opportunities, systemically-determined social emergencies, lack of public facilities, and so on. Therefore, "poverty" is defined not merely as a lack of material resources but as "capability deprivation," in which human beings are deprived of the freedom to lead a decent and dignified life (Sen [2000]).

Indeed, such a viewpoint has to be developed as a public ethics in order to restore the suffering peoples and disaster-stricken areas. Moreover, the ethics of care for the suffering peoples, especially for children and old persons, is indispensable. These requirements for public ethics mean that we require the three-dimensional ethics described in Chapter 2; i.e., *duty ethics, virtue ethics, and ethics of positive/negative values*.

---

[10] See Rawls [1971], Walzer [1983], and Sandel [1982].

[11] See Kaldor [2007].

5.5.2 Eco-philosophical Integration of Three-dimensional Ethics for Future Generations

The ethics after nuclear disaster must include an element for future generations, which the naïve dream of progress by the development of technology and big sciences criticizes. In this regard, the eco-philosophers described above (5.4) are especially remarkable. Therefore, it is important to *combine their views with our advocacy of the integration of three-dimensional public ethics*, which I described at the end of Chapter 2.

Hans Jonas' *The Imperative of Responsibility,* which can be regarded as a pioneering masterpiece on ethics for future generations, clearly belongs to the *duty-based ethics* derived from Kant, while its ontology opposes the Kantian dualism of mind and nature. Jonas states that human survival is the unconditional duty of all humankind. This is expressed in the following categorical imperative:

> "Act so that the effects of your action are compatible with the permanence of genuine human life"; or expressed negatively: "Act so that the effects of your action are not destructive of the future possibility of such life"; or simply: "Do not compromise the conditions for an indefinite continuation of humanity on earth"; or, again turned positive: "In your present choices, include the future wholeness of Man among the object of your will."
>
> (Jonas [1979], [1984] Chap. I-Vff.)

It is particularly important in this respect to be constantly aware of the "worst-case scenario" and to approach the linked questions "What can we do?" and "What should we do?" accordingly. Jonas suggests that the duty to future generations should be seen in the same way as the obligation of parents to support their children (ibid. Chap. 4-IIIff.).

In my view, this kind of ethics for future generations is very powerful and important, but it requires more space for virtue ethics. As I stated at the end of Chapter 2, duty is an important component of ethics but may convey too strict an impression to the people. Public ethics for future generations will probably only attain greater vitality through *virtue ethics for the citizen*, which is centered on spontaneous or responsive human behavior, as well as on *Phronesis* (practical wisdom), in each situation, rather than the categorical imperative (Aristotle [2013]). It also requires space for the ethics and politics of *positive and negative values*, such as nuclear power, alternative energies, nuclear waste, and the decommissioning of nuclear power plants. In this regard, the deliberative democracy among citizens would play a great role.

In contrast to Jonas, Imamichi's eco-ethica places too much emphasis on virtue ethics. As I described above, it emphasizes traditional virtues such as courage, loyalty, humility, and responsibility, and the new virtues such as love of strangers (*philoxenia*), punctuality, cosmopolitanism, mastery of languages and equipment, mental diversion (*eutrapelia*), etc., which must be learned by everyone (Imamichi [2009] pp. 33ff.). His remarkable idea seems, however, to lack a public policy based on duty ethics. As a matter of fact, Imamichi himself wished to take a distance from the political world. Still, this stance is too romantic to gain public power. Imamichi's excellent idea must therefore be developed in a more public-philosophical way, together with public policy based upon duty-oriented ethics.

In this regard, Spaemann's abovementioned eco-philosophy that integrates duty ethics, virtue ethics, and public value ethics seems more plausible; even for people who do not share his belief in Catholic Christianity. In any event, it will be our task to develop a three-dimensional ethics for the future generations.

5.6 *Glocal Hope and Responsibility* after Fukushima, Hiroshima, and Nagasaki

I would like to conclude this chapter by advancing *glocal hope and responsibility*; not only after the Fukushima disaster but after Hiroshima and Nagasaki as well.

Apart from philosophers, it should be pointed out that there are some exceptional natural scientists in postwar Japan who have been objecting to nuclear power politics. Among them, the activities of the abovementioned late Jinzaburō Takagi (高木仁三郎) stand out, and I re-appreciate Takagi in this last section. Since *glocal* philosophy attaches much importance to a *trans-disciplinary viewpoint*, I take up here his *positive vision* for our future after the Fukushima disaster.

As a professional authority on nuclear chemistry, Takagi warned the Japanese people of the dangers of nuclear power and advocated the conversion from atomic civilization to a more peaceful form of living. According to him, it is hardly possible for us to live with nuclear power, because such power is accompanied by a lot of dangers, risks, and costs. It is also a great mistake for us to think that nuclear waste can be recycled. Takagi criticized the members of the nuclear village, because they showed no public mindedness and even confused this with governmental orders. If they really had a public mind, they would not conceal any of the risks of nuclear power from the Japanese people.

Takagi tried to develop scientific research for the Japanese public, but, unfortunately, he passed away due to the cancer in 2000. It was not until the Fukushima accident over 10 years later that his warning turned out to be true. In his final years, Takagi outlined what he considered to be the ideal society and world as follows.

First, it must be a society in which the relationship not only among human beings but also between *human beings and nature* is not oppressive.

Second, it must be a society in which all people are guaranteed to *live peacefully*.

Third, it must be a *just and fair* society.

Fourth, *the world*, which consists of such societies, must *sustain forever*.

(Takagi [2000] pp. 239-250)

Based upon this ideal vision, Takagi tried to draft a radical statement about the "disarmament of science and technology" to scientists, as well as to the general public, all over the world. This meant a requirement for the "change of civilization from an atomic one to another one." Interestingly enough, he did not to forget to emphasize the *value of hope* to the future. He criticized the pessimistic tendency of the peace movement in postwar Japan because it lacked *the philosophy of hope* and made a poor impression on Japanese people, as it seemingly only conducted a negative campaign against nuclear powers. Instead of such a gloomy movement, he stressed the *value of hope* and attached much importance to opening up a *responsible and hopeful route to the future generation*; not only in terms of peace but also in terms of human rights and environmental preservation. Thus, at least in my view, he was a *public philosopher on science and technology*, and we should take up his pioneering achievements and develop our public mind so as to seek an alternative to nuclear civilization.

In my view, this is a statement of public philosophy, although Takagi was not a philosopher but a natural scientist. This means that *natural scientists as well as technologists must become public philosophers as far as they are public citizens*. The ontology of *multi-dimensional, responsive, and becoming Self* should be shared among scientists and technologists. What is important here is also to integrate *the tripartite method of learning through interdisciplinary collaboration* in which each philosopher, social scientist, natural scientist technologist, and even physician takes part in his or her own way. The integration of *three-dimensional public ethics* should be activated among citizens, too.

This makes not only "the movement away from nuclear power" welcome but also the declaration of intent by President Obama of the United States to abolish all nuclear weapons. This is something that particularly concerns the Japanese, who have experienced Hiroshima, Nagasaki, and Fukushima. Indeed, it is truly important for the Japanese people and government to make efforts to abolish nuclear weapons and nuclear power, even though the present situation remains far from this goal. In my view, this is our *glocal hope and responsibility* for future generations and for peaceful civilization. We should break away from the stress of nuclear civilization and direct our steps toward a *peaceful nuclear-free civilization* with the strong *democratic governance of civil society and government* to perform this heavy task.

6 Re-conceptualizing *WA* (和) for the Culture of World Peace

In this last chapter, I try to renew the concept of *WA* (和) on the basis of *glocal* public philosophy for the culture of world peace. In my view, this attempt is very important for two reasons. One reason is that this concept can be seen as a *glocal message from Japan, as well as Northeast Asian countries,* to the people all over the world. The second is that it suggests the integration of peace, justice, human rights, and solidarity based upon *glocal* ontology, as well as public ethics, in the *trans-national civil society*.

In ordinary Japanese, *WA* (和) as an adjective is typically used to describe things that are especially Japanese, such as Washoku (和食Japanese cuisine) or Washitsu (和室a Japanese room). The usage of the separate adjectives *WA* (Japanese和), *KAN* (Chinese漢), and *YOH* (Europe 洋), indicates nothing other than that the Japanese make a distinction between Japanese, Chinese, and European. However, *WA* is not and should not be confined to this meaning.

Starting from this premise, I would like first to re-conceptualize *WA* as a *transnational public value* that originates from Confucianism and Buddhism, exercising much influence on Japanese cultures. Referring to contemporary public philosophies, I will then show that *WA* could be a very important transnational public value for world peace, justice, human rights, and solidarity.

6.1 A Short History of the Concept of *WA* in China and Japan

I begin by recollecting the traditional meaning of this idea in China and Japan.

6.1.1 Chinese Tradition

First, I will discuss *WA* (和 harmony) as distinct from *DOH* (同 sameness) in the ancient Chinese tradition. In fact, *WA* and *DOH* are as different from each other as chalk and cheese. In the ancient Chinese tradition, the best known proverb is *WAshite Dohzezu* (和して同ぜず) written in the *Analects of Confucius* (論語子路): a very famous Confucian classic. I would like to translate this proverb as "a public spiritual person who harmonizes without assimilating." This means that the public spiritual individual communicates with those who have different opinions and tries to harmonize with them based on his or her just and fair mind; however, this individual does not assimilate with them or force them to assimilate in return. This is in contrast to narrow-minded people who easily assimilate with others without much thought but never harmonize with one another.

According to *Zuo zhuan* (春秋左氏伝), one of the Chinese Historical Classics, *WA* harmonizes various flavors such as hot, sour, sweet, salty, and bitter, as well as various ingredients, in order to cook delicious soup, whereas *DOH* gathers only one flavor or ingredient. This parable is also valid in thinking about the relationship between the king and the subject. That is to say, *DOH* is the attitude of a subject who serves as a "yes-man" and obeys his king blindly or uncritically. In contrast to this, *WA* is the attitude of the subject who is ready to point out wrong or unjust components of the king's thought and prompt him to change them into "right or just things." Only based upon relationships led by *WA* could human beings live peacefully and the conflicts among various peoples vanish (*Zuo zhuan* 昭公 20).

According to *Guo-yu* (国語), which is also one of the famous Chinese Classics, *WA* has something to do with "development and generativity" (*Guo-yu* Vol.16. 鄭語). *WA* means, namely, the principle of making it possible for something to develop or generate other things, while *DOH* has no such a capability.

In this way, *WA* in Chinese tradition was understood, in contrast to *DOH*, as a dynamic principle for *peaceful and just harmony and development*.

6.1.2 Japanese Tradition

How was this concept developed in Japanese tradition? I will briefly comment on this question.

In Japanese tradition, *WA* (和) has been used as the meaning of harmony and peace since the time of *Shōtoku Taishi* (聖徳太子 c. 574-622). He advanced a *Constitution comprising 17 Articles*, and Article 1 declares that *WA (Harmony) is to be valued*.

According to Nakamura Hajime, whose thought I have described in Chapter 3, Shōtoku Taishi was strongly influenced by Buddhism; especially by the idea of "benevolence and compassion." Against the narrow interpretation that Shōtoku Taishi's Constitution was nothing but compliance with governmental officials, Nakamura interprets it as an ethics for all Japanese rulers. *WA* is meant as a principle of harmonious activity; not only within a group but also among various groups. Pointing out the similarity of *Shōtoku* to *Asoka* in India, Nakamura regards Article 17 as the beginning of the democratic mindset in Japanese history. Although Article 2 states, "one should not disobey orders," he rejects its interpretation as the order of obedience and instead regards it a principle for harmonious human relations in each group. He also rejects the interpretation that *WA* in Article 1 denies argumentation and individuality. On the contrary, he considers that it respects each individual in each group (Nakamura [1998] pp. 89ff).

In my view, Nakamura's radical reinterpretation is very suggestive for our re-conceptualization of world peace. Still, I cannot but point out that *WA* (和) in Japanese history tended to be confounded with *DOH*; i.e., with conformity or behaving similarly. In spite of Nakamura's favorable interpretation, even the Article in Shōtoku Taishi's Constitution, "one should not disobey orders," connotes *DOH*, because uncritical obedience sometimes tends to force people into assimilation. If this is the case, the spirit of *WA* could easily be transformed into the spirit of *DOH*.

Generally speaking, although there are a few Japanese thinkers such as *Ogyū Sorai* (荻生徂徠 1666-1728) who were influenced by Confucianism and emphasized the distinction between *WA* and *DOH* (Ogyū [1987/1716-36] pp. 218-219), such a distinction has not received so much attention in modern Japan. As a matter of fact, this meaning (implying conformity) played a totalitarian role in modern Japanese history, as "the Cardinal Principles of the National Polity" issued by the Ministry of Education in 1937 showed. Emphasizing *WA* as a collectivist virtue of Japanese culture in contrast to Western individualism, these Principles played an ideological role in driving many innocent Japanese people to WWII. There is no denying that the concept of *WA* then degenerated from a transnational public value into a totalitarian nationalist ideology.

As I stressed in the previous chapters, however, Japan became a peaceful society on the basis of a new Japanese Constitution and Fundamental Law of Education, although some reactionary people have rejected them. Therefore, the notion of *WA* must be re-conceptualized as a *trans-national comprehensive public value* for a world peace that includes justice, human rights, and solidarity.

6.2 *WA* as a Trans-national Public Value Based upon *Restorative* Justice

First, I would like to stress that the notion of *WA* should be understood as a very important trans-national public value for the mutual understanding of various cultures in the world. The current globalization tends to produce a homogenization of cultures; i.e., *DOH* on the one hand, and disharmonies, conflicts, and terrorism (including WAR) on the other hand. This tendency must be absolutely criticized and reoriented by the concept of *WA*, which produces mutual recognition and understanding of various cultures against cultural ethnocentrism, closed nationalism, homogeneous globalism, and all kinds of war.

It would be too optimistic, however, to think that we could perform the logic of *WA* without regard to the history of the past. Regrettably, the history of humankind has not been oriented by the idea of *WA*, which recognizes cultural differences such as languages, religions, social customs, and so on. On the contrary, humankind has been marred by misunderstandings, conflicts, and even the instigation of wars. Therefore, we need the second key concept *Wakai* (和解), which means *reconciliation and restorative justice*.

Indeed, we should understand the concept of *WA* not only as *Harmony in Diversity and Differences* but also as *Peace Based upon Reconciliation* (和解). As a matter of fact, when we look up the word *WA* (和) in the Japanese-English dictionary, we can find English equivalents such as "peace," "harmony," and even sometimes "reconciliation" (NEW SUNRISE *Japanese-English Dictionary* [1993] Obunsha, Tokyo). We should make use of these translations for re-conceptualizing *WA*, embracing all such meanings as a transversal value on the global level.

In this regard, we need the idea of *restorative justice*, to which I already referred in Chapter 1. This idea stands in contrast to "retaliatory or retributive notions of justice" such as "an eye for an eye; a tooth for a tooth." That is to say, *restorative justice* aims not at revenge but instead at apology and forgiveness. It requires us to admit the undeniable historical facts and errors of the past, to co-memorize them in the present, and to have the strong will to overcome this negative legacy and construct common values in the future (De Gruchy [2002]). Without such historical and temporal elements, there can be no restorative justice.

As I have stressed repeatedly, the public world has not only a spatial-present dimension but a temporal-historical dimension. Therefore, it would be a great challenge for public philosophy to address how to deal with the past, present, and future of the trans-national public world of human beings based upon restorative justice.

6.3 *WA* as a Trans-national Value for *Positive* Peace and Human Rights

Now, I would like to enlarge the concept of *WA*, which originally means peace and harmony among the people, to the level of world peace and human rights

As I said in Chapter 1, there are two notions of peace: one is *negative peace* that means the absent of overt violent conflict, and the other is *positive peace* that includes a range of relationships up to a point where nations (or any groupings in conflict) might engage in collaborative and supportive relationships. Both relate to *human rights*. The former relates, however, mainly to the right to living safely, and enables a world akin to Hobbes' Leviathan [1958/1651]). However, any other human rights such as freedom of speech, expression, and academic thought cannot always be guaranteed in this state. It is important to point out that Leviathan is based upon the fear of state authority, as well as upon a distrust of human nature, and this cannot be compatible with the idea of *WA*. That is why we must combine *WA* as a very important trans-national value with the notion of *positive peace*.

In my view, the classic notion of positive peace was defined clearly by Spinoza, who stated that "peace is not the lack of war, but a virtue arising from the spiritual power of the people" (Spinoza [1958] p. 311). He believed that the peaceful world is constructed by the power of reasonable people, who are driven by hope rather than by fear. Moreover, he emphasized that harmonious collaboration among the people is indispensable. Thus, his conception of *positive* peace corresponds with our idea of *WA*.

How does positive peace relate to social justice and human rights?

As I introduced in Chapter 1, Johan Galtung, who is an enthusiastic advocate of positive peace, emphasizes the close relationship of positive peace and human rights. According to him, positive peace indicates the state in which there is no structural violence, and positive peace thus cannot be realized without eliminating such structural violence; i.e., without realizing human rights in the sense of both economic-social and civil-political rights, as the *International Covenants on Human Rights* (1966, 1976) declare (Galtung [1996]).

We have to connect this notion with the contemporary public philosophy for human rights.

Since John Rawls advanced *A Theory of Justice* in 1971, the concept of justice has been closely connected with human rights; at least in the scholarly world. As I have described in Chapter 2, this new concept of justice consists of each person's equal right to equal basic liberties (first principle), and the arrangement of social and economic inequalities so that they are both of the greatest benefit to the least advantaged and attached to offices and positions open to all under conditions of fair equality of opportunity (second principle). We can regard the first principle as civil and political human rights, and the second principle as economic and social rights.

Rawls' theory of justice is connected with the theory of human rights, however, rather than the theory of peace. Interestingly, Rawls later book, *The Law of Peoples*, treated world peace without discussing global justice. Against Thomas Pogge and Charles Beitz, who try to apply Rawls' concept of justice on the global level, Rawls in this book advocated the peaceful collaboration between liberal societies and decent illiberal non-democratic hierarchical societies without applying his theory of justice to this context (Rawls [1999]).

I do not go into details about controversies regarding this book. Instead, I would like to state that Rawls was partly right in that he tried to avoid a kind of Anglo-American-centric cultural imperialism, which prefers liberal rights to economic and social rights. At the same time, I believe that Rawls was wrong in that he abandoned any potential theory of trans-national human rights that might realize positive peace by people all over the world. His *The Law of Peoples* remains at the level of *negative peace*, except that he admits humanitarian intervention into the outlaw states. The public philosophy for human rights, together with the public philosophy for *solidarity*, can overcome this weakness.

6.4 *WA* as *Trans-national Solidarity* Based upon *Compassion*

Now, I would like to stress that the idea of *WA* for world peace and human rights must be reinforced by a *transnational value of solidarity* among the peoples all over the world. As a matter of fact, the theory of world peace and human rights would be powerless unless put into practice by the people's power. That is why we need solidarity among people in order to attain world peace and human rights.

WA, when written as 輪in Japanese, has the meaning of *circle*, which can express the solidarity of the people. When used as verb, it can mean "mitigating" (和らげる) the mind and body of suffering people. Therefore, I would like to orient the concept of *WA toward transnational solidarity* (連帯の輪) *with suffering people* on the basis of the public ethics and *glocal* ontology described in the previous chapters.

As was shown previously, public ethics in our sense consists of duty, virtue, and public values/negative values, and *glocal* ontology consists of our *multi-dimensional, dialogical, and becoming understanding of Self, Others, and Public World*. When we think about trans-national solidarity for world peace and human rights in view of the contemporary world, however, *public reason is not enough*; even though it means, contrary to the narrow understanding by Rawls (who limited it to the level of governmental officials), the reason shared by the people. I mean that other capacities such as *public compassion and public imaginations must be added to public reason* and thereby strengthen our idea of trans-national public ethics and *glocal* ontology.

Indeed, public values such as peace, justice, and human rights must be not only recognized by reason but also felt and perceived on the level of sympathy, while negative values that cause suffering to people all over the world could and must be understood on the level of compassion rather than reason. In this regard, Schopenhauer's ethics of solidarity based upon compassion among the people is very inspiring.

Differing from Nietzsche, who advocated *Zarathustra* to escape the nihilism and contempt of the secular world, Schopenhauer advocated solidarity based on compassion so as to overcome the sorrowful world. He even regarded it as the same as the love for one's neighbors in the sense of Christianity (Schopenhauer [1972/1858] Vol.4.§ 66-67), while he seemed to be influenced by the Buddhist idea of *compassion* (慈悲) to which Nakamura Hajime paid much importance in his understanding of *WA* (as shown above). In this regard, *WA* that refers to *solidarity* (輪) and connotes *compassion* (慈悲) could play a very important role in solidarity with suffering people. Corresponding to this, *WA* in Japanese as an intransitive verb (yawaragu, 和らぐ, nagomu, 和む) means "soften," "ease," "thaw," "moderate," "relax," "melt," "be mitigated," etc. *WA* as a transitive verb (yawarageru, 和らげる) means "mitigate," soften," "cushion," "ease," "melt," and even "disarm." Thus, *WA* in this sense could relate to compassion and solidarity with suffering people.

Indeed, the value of compassion becomes more and more important after the tragic event of September 11, 2001, and March 11, 2011, as well as the Syrian refugee problem in 2015 and war and terrorism all over the world. In such a catastrophic situation, we need a *trans-national solidarity based on compassion*. Thus, *WA* as solidarity based upon compassion strengthens our idea of trans-national public ethics and *glocal* ontology, which consists of a multi-dimensional, dialogical, and becoming Self in opposition to a one-dimensional, dogmatic, and inflexible Self.

A Very Short Concluding Remark

As is widely known, the famous Preamble to the *UNESCO Constitution* declares, "Since wars begin in the minds of men, it is the minds of men that the defenses of peace must be constructed."

When ethically re-conceptualized in terms of *Harmony* (Chowa 調和), *Peace* (Heiwa平和), *Reconciliation* (Wakai 和解), *Mitigation* (Yawarageru和らげる), and *Solidarity* (人間の輪), *WA* as a trans-national comprehensive value can contribute to the construction of defenses of peace in the mind. This can then generate *the peace-building gentle human solidarity for mitigating the suffering of people all over the world* (人々の苦悩を和らげる柔和な平和のための連帯の輪), which marks a sharp contrast to "WAR."

References

Anders, Günther [1995] *Hiroshima ist überall*, München: C.H. Beck.

Adorno, Theodor [1973/1966] *Negative Dialektik,* Frankfurt am Main: Suhrkamp.

— [1983/1955] *Prisms,* translated by Sherry Nicholson and Samuel Weber, Cambridge, Massachusetts: MIT Press.

Adorno, Theodor, and Horkheimer, Max [1969/1947] *Dialektik der Aufklärung*, Frankfurt am Main: Suhrkamp.

Arendt, Hannah [1958] *The Human Condition,* Chicago: The University of Chicago Press.

Aristotle [1996] *The Politics and the Constitution of Athens*, edited by Stephen Everson, Cambridge: Cambridge UP.

— [2000] *Nicomachean Ethics*, edited by Roger Crisp, Cambridge: Cambridge UP.

Bacon, Francis [1963/1605] *Advancement of Learning*, London: Everyman's Library.

Barshay, Andrew [1988] *State and Intellectual in Imperial Japan: The Public Man in Crisis*, Berkeley: University of California Press.

Beck, Urlich [1986] *Risikogesellschaft: Auf dem Weg in eine andere Moderne*, Frankfurt am Main: Suhrkamp.

Beitz, Charles R. [1979] *Political Theory and International Relations*, Princeton, NJ: Princeton UP.

Bellah, Robert [1991] *The Good Society*, New York: Alfred A. Knopf.

— [2003] *Imagining Japan: The Japanese Tradition and Its Modern Interpretation* Berkeley: University of California Press.

— [2014] *Religion and Global Society* (*Shukyo to Global Shakai* in Japanese), edited by Shimazono Susumu and Okumura Takashi, Tokyo: Iwanami.

Bellah, Robert, et al. [1985] *Habits of the Heart: Individualism and Commitment in American Life,* Berkeley: University of California Press.

Berque, Augustin [2006] "From Watsuji's concept of 'human' to beyond the limits of modern ontological topos," in Wauchope, Samantha(ed.) *Cultural Diversity and Transversal Values: East-West Dialogue on Spiritual and Secular Dynamics*. Paris: UNESCO, pp. 138-144.

Calhoun, Craig (ed.) [1992] *Habermas and the Public Sphere,* Cambridge, Massachusetts: The MIT Press.

Calichmann, Richard F. (ed.) [2008] *Overcoming Modernity: Cultural Identity in Wartime Japan,* New York: Columbia UP.

Canovan, Margaret [1994] *Hannah Arendt: A Reinterpretation of Her Political Thought*, Cambridge: Cambridge UP.

Carr, Edward Hallett [1964/1961] *What Is History?*, London: Penguin Books.

Carter, Robert E. [2013] *The Kyoto School: An Introduction*, New York: SUNY Press.

Commission on Human Security (ed.) [2003] *Human Security Now*, New York: United Nations Publications.

Condorcet, Antoine Nicolas [2009/1795] *Outlines of an Historical View of the Progress of the Human Mind,* Chicago: G. Langer.

Dahrendorf, Ralf [1992] *Der moderne soziale Konflikt. Essay zur Politik der Freiheit.* Stuttgart: Deutsche Verlags-Anstalt.

De Gruchy, John W. [2002] *Reconciliation: Restoring Justice*, Minneapolis: Fortress Press.
Dewey, John [1954/1927] *The Public and Its Problems,* Athens: Ohio UP.
Eisenstadt, Shmuel Noah [2002] *Multiple Modernities*, New Brunswick, New Jersey: Transaction Publishers.
Ferguson, Adam [1995/1767] *An Essay on the History of Civil Society*, New Brunswick, New Jersey: Transaction Publishers.
Fichte, Johann Gottlieb [2012/1806] *Die Anweisung zum seligen Leben oder auch die Religionslehre*, Hamburg: Felix Meiner Verlag.
— [1978/1808] *Reden an die Deutsche Nation*, Hamburg: Felix Meiner Verlag.
Foljanty-Jost, Gesine, and Hüstebeck, Momoyo (eds.) [2013] *Bürger und Staat in Japan,* Halle: Universitätsverlag Halle-Wittenberg.
Fukuda Tokuzō [2015/1922] *Social Policy and Class Struggle (Shakai Seisaku to Kaikyū Tōsō* in Japanese) Tokyo: Shinzansha.
— [1980/1930]*Welfare Economy (Kosei Keizai* in Japanse) Tokyo: Kodansha.
Fukuyama, Francis [2006/1990] *The End of History and the Last Man*, New York: Free Press.
Fukuzawa, Yukichi [1963/1872-76] *An Encouragement of Learning*, translated, with an introduction, by David A. Dilworth and Umeyo Hirano, Tokyo: Sophia University (Monumenta Nipponica monographs).
— [1978/1872-76] *An Encouragement of Learning (Gakumon no Susume* in Japanese), Tokyo: Iwanami.
— [1973/1875] *An Outline of a Theory of Civilization*, translated by David A Dilworth and G. Cameron Hurst, Tokyo: Sophia University (Monumenta Nipponica monographs, UNESCO collection of representative works; Japanese series).
— [1995/1875] *An Outline of a Theory of Civilization (Bunmeiron no Gairyaku* in Japanese), Tokyo: Iwanami.
Gadamer, Hans-Georg [1960] *Wahrheit und Methode*, Tübingen: Mohr.
— [1996/1979] *Philosophische Lehrjahre: Eine Rückschau* (*Tetsugakushugyoujidai*, Japanese Translation) Tokyo: Miraisha.
Galtung, Johan [1996] *Peace by Peaceful Means: Peace and Conflict, Development and Civilization*, London: Sage Publishing Ltd.
Goodin, Robert E. [1995] *Utilitarianism as a Public Philosophy*, Cambridge: Cambridge UP.
Gordon, Andrew [2013] *A Modern History of Japan: From Tokugawa Times to the Present,* Oxford: Oxford UP.
Habermas, Jürgen [1990/1962] *Strukturwandel der Öffentlichkeit,* Frankfurt am Main: Suhrkamp.
— [1981] *Theorie des kommunikativen Handelns, Vols.1, 2*, Frankfurt am Main: Suhrkamp.
— [1981/1980] "Die Moderne – ein unvollendetes Projekt," in *Kleine Politische Schriften I-IV*, Frankfurt am Main: Suhrkamp, pp.444-464.
— [1991] *Erläuterungen zur Diskursethik*, Frankfurt am Main: Suhrkamp.
— [2011] *Zur Verfassung Europas, Ein Essay*, Berlin: Suhrkamp.
Hegel, George Wilhelm Friedrich [1952/1807] *Phänomenologie des Geistes*, Hamburg: Felix Meiner Verlag.

— [1969/1832] *Vorlesung über die Philosophie der Religion*, Frankfurt am Main: Suhrkamp.

— [1970/1821] *Grundlinien der Philosophie des Rechts*, Frankfurt am Main: Suhrkamp.

— [1970/1840] *Vorlesungen über die Philosophie der Geschichte,* Frankfurt am Main: Suhrkamp.

— [1998-99/1830] *Enzyklopädie der philosophischen Wissenschaften im Grundrisse*, 3 Vols., Frankfurt am Main: Suhrkamp.

Heidegger, Martin [1977/1927] *Sein und Zeit*, Frankfurt am Main: Vittorio Klostermann.

— [2014] *4 Abteilungen Überlegung: Schwarze Hefte 1931-1938*, Frankfurt am Main: Vittorio Klostermann.

Hirata, Kiyoaki [1969] *Bourgeois Society and Socialism* (*Shimin Shakai to Shakai Shugi* in Japanese) Tokyo: Iwanami

Hiromatsu, Wataru [1989] *An Essay on the Overcoming of Modernity – A Critical Stance on the History of Ideas in the Showa Period* (*"Kindai no Chōkoku" ron* in Japanese), Tokyo: Kodansha.

— [1991] *The Intersubjective and Ontological Structure of the World* (*Sekai no Kyodo Shyukanteki Sonzai Kouzou* in Japanese), Tokyo: Kodansha.

— [1996] *The Collected Works, Vols. 14-16* (in Japanese), Tokyo: Iwanami.

— [1996/1993] *Being and Meaning: A Foundation to the World of Things* (*Sonzai to Imi: Kototeki Sekaikan no Teiso* in Japanese), in *The Collected Papers, Vols. 15-16*, Tokyo: Iwanami.

Hobbes, Thomas [1958/1651] *Leviathan*, Oxford: Clarendon Press.

Horkheimer, Max [1992/1937] *Traditionelle und kritische Theorie: Fünf Aufsätze* Frankfurt am Main: Fischer Taschenbuch.

— [1981/1961] "Die Aktualität Schopenhauers,"in *Über Arthur Schopenhauer,* edited by Gerd Haffmans, 3. Auflage, Zurich: Diogenes Taschenbuch, S. 159.

Huntington, Samuel [1996] *The Clash of Civilizations and the Remaking of World Order,* New York: Simon & Schuster.

Imamichi, Tomonobu [2009] *An Introduction to Eco-Ethica*, translated by Judy Wakabayashi, Lanham, Maryland: University Press of America.

Ishibashi, Tanzan [1984/1912-1968] *Essays in Criticism (Hyōronshū* in Japanese) Tokyo: Iwanami.

Izutsu, Toshihiko [1991/1981] *What is the Islamic Culture? (Isuramu Bunka Towa Nanika* in Japanese), Tokyo: Iwanami.

— [1983] *Consciousness and Substance: Searching for the Spiritual East* (*Ishiki to Honshitsu* in Japanese), Tokyo: Iwanami.

— [1992] *The Collected Papers 9* (in Japanese) Tokyo: Chuokoronsha.

— [2001] *Toward a Philosophy of Zen Buddhism*, Boulder, Colorado: Prajna.

— [2002] *Ethico-Religious Concepts in the Qur'an,* Montreal: McGill-Queen's UP.

Jonas, Hans [1966] *The Phenomenon of Life: Toward a Phenomenological Biology,* Evanston, Illinois: Northwestern University Press.

— [1979] *Das Prinzip der Verantwortung: Versuch einer Ethik für die technologische Zivilization*, Frankfurt am Main: Insel.

— [1984/1979] *The Imperative of Responsibility: In Search of an Ethics for the Technological Age*, Chicago: The University of Chicago Press.

— [2003] *Erinnerungen*, Frankfurt am Main: Insel.

Jung-Sun N. Han [2012] *An Imperial Path to Modernity – Yoshino Sakuzo and a New Liberal Order in East Asia, 1905-1937*, Cambridge, Massachusetts: Harvard University Asia Center.

Kaldor, Mary [2007], *Human Security*, Cambridge: Polity Press.

Kant, Immanuel [1964/1785] "Beantwortung der Frage: Was ist Aufklärung?" in *Werke in zwölf Bänden XI*, Frankfurt am Main: Suhrkamp/Insel, pp. 53-61.

— [1972/1795] *Zum ewigen Frieden*, Stuttgart: Reclam.

— [1959/1798] *Der Streit der Fakultäten*, Hamburg: Felix Meiner Verlag.

— [1970] *Political Writings*, edited by Hans Reiss, Cambridge: Cambridge UP.

Kaul, Inge, Grünberg, Isabelle, and Stern, Marc A. (eds.) [1999] *Global Public Goods: International Cooperation in the 21st Century,* Oxford: Oxford UP.

Keane, John [1998] *Civil Society: Old Images and New Visions*, Cambridge: Polity Press.

— [2003] *Global Civil Society?* Cambridge: Cambridge UP.

Keys, Mary [2008] *Aquinas, Aristotle, and the Promise of the Common Good*, Cambridge: Cambridge UP.

Komatsu, Yutaka [2011] *Genuine Civilization Never Kills the People* (*Shin no Bunmei wa Hito o Korosazu* in Japanese), Tokyo: Shogakukan.

— [2013] *Tanaka, Shōzō: A Public Intellectual for the Future* (*Tanaka, Shōzō – Mirai no Tsumugu Chisikijin* in Japanese), Tokyo: Iwanami.

Kōtoku Shūsui [2008/1901], *L'impérialisme, le spectre du vingtième siècle*, traduction, annotation et introduction par Christine Lévy, Paris: CNRS.

Kraft, Victor [1968/1950] *Der Wiener Kreis: Der Ursprung des Neopositivismus Ein Kapitel der jüngsten Philosophiegeschichte,* Vienna/New York: Springer.

Lippmann, Walter [1987/1922] *Public Opinion,* New York: Free Press.

— [1993/1925] *Phantom Public*, New Brunswick, New Jersey: Transaction Publishers.

— [1989/1955] *The Public Philosophy*, New Brunswick, New Jersey: Transaction Publishers.

Lukács, George [2013/1923] *Geschichte und Klassenbewußtsein,* Bielefeld: Aisthesis Verlag; Neuauflage.

— [1954] *Die Zerströng der Vernunft*, Berlin (East): Aufbau-Verlag.

Lyotard, Jean-François [1979] *La condition postmoderne*, Paris: Minuit.

— [1983] *Le Differend*, Paris: Edition de Minuit.

MacIntyre, Alasdair [1981] *After Virtue: A Study in Moral Theory*, Indiana: University of Notre Dame Press.

— [1988] *Whose Justice, Which Rationality?* Indiana: University of Notre Dame Press.

Maruyama, Masao [1995-96 Vol.3/1941] *Studies in the Intellectual History of Tokugawa Japan* (*Nihon Seiji Shiso Shi Kenkyu* in Japanese) Tokyo: Iwanami.

— [2008/1974] *Studies in the Intellectual History of Tokugawa Japan*, translated by Mikiso Hane, New York: ACLS History E-Book Project.

— [1964/1957-58] *Thought and Behavior in Modern Japanese Politics (Gendai Seiji no Shiso to Kodo, Expanded Edition* in Japanese), Tokyo: Miraisha.

— [2008/1963] *Thought and Behavior in Modern Japanese Politics (Expanded Edition),* translated by Ivan Morris, New York: ACLS History E-Book Project.

— [1961] *Thinking in Japan* (*Nihon no Shiso* in Japanese), Tokyo: Iwanami.

— [2012 /1961] *Denken in Japan*, translated by Wolfgang Schamoni and Wolfgang Seifert, Berlin: Suhrkamp.

— [1965] "Patterns of Individuation and the Case of Japan" in: Marius B. Jansen (ed.) *Changing Japanese attitude Modernization*, New Jersey: Princeton UP. pp.489-531.
— [1982] *From the Rearguard (Koei no Ichi kara* in Japanese), Tokyo: Miraisha.
— [2001/1942-1992] *Philosophy of Fukuzawa Yukichi* (*Fukuzawa Yukichi no Tetsugaku* in Japanese), edited by Matsuzawa Hiroaki, Tokyo: Iwanami.
— [2006] *Review of my Past Life, vol.2* (*Kaikodan* in Japanese), edited by Matsuzawa Hiroaki and Uete Michiari, Tokyo: Iwanami.
Merleau-Ponty, Maurice [1945] *Phénoménologie de la perception*, Paris: Gallimard.
Miki, Kiyoshi [1980/1926] *A Study on Human Being in Pascal* (*Pascal ni Okeru Ningen no Kenkyu* in Japanese), Tokyo: Iwanami.
— [1966-68/1928-39] *The Complete Works Vols. 3, 5, 10, 16, 17* (in Japanese), Tokyo: Iwanami.
Minamoto, Ryoen [2005] "Yokoi Shonan's Concept of Kaikoku (Opening the Country/ The Open Country) and the Foundation of the Concept of the Public," in *Transactions of the Japanese Academy*, 57(3).
Miyazaki, Tōten [1982/1902] *My Thirty-Three Year's Dream*, translated, with an introduction, by Eto Shinkichi and Marius B. Jansen, Princeton UP.
— [1993/1902] *My Thirty-Three Year's' Dream* (*Sanjyu Sannen no Yume* in Japanese), Tokyo: Iwanami.
Najita, Tetsuo [1974] "Some Reflections on Idealism in the Political Thought of Yoshino Sakuzo," in Silberman, Bernard S., and Harootunian, H.D. (eds.) *Japan in Crisis*, New Jersey: Princeton UP. pp.29-66.
Nakae, Chōmin [1984/1882-1901] *Collected Papers* (in Japanese), Tokyo: Chuokoronsha.
— [1965/1887] *Discourse by Three Drunkards on Government* (*Sansuijin Keirin Mondo* in Japanese), Tokyo: Iwanami.
— [1984/1887] A Discourse by Three Drunkards on Government, translated by Nobuko Tsukui and Jeffrey Hammond, Tokyo and New York: Weatherhill.
— [2008/1887] *Dialogues politiques entre trois ivrognes*, traduction, annotation et introduction par Christine Lévy et Eddy Dufourmont, Paris: Éditions du CNRS.
Nakamura, Hajime [2010/1955] *Jihi* (in Japanese), Tokyo: Kodansha.
— [1964] *Ways of Thinking of Eastern People: India, China, Tibet, Japan*. Hawaii: University of Hawaii Press.
— [1985] *The Mind in Eastern Cultures* (*Toyo no Kokoro* in Japanese), Tokyo: Kodansha.
— [1998] *Shōtoku Taishi* (in Japanese) Tokyo: Shunjyusha.
— [2004] *Sayings in Buddhist Literature* (*Butten no Kotoba* in Japanese), Tokyo: Kodansha.
Nanbara, Shigeru [2014/1942] *State and Religion* (*Kokka to Syukyo* in Japanese), Tokyo: Iwanami.
— [1959] *Fichte's Political Philosophy* (*Fichte no Seiji Tetsugaku* in Japanese), Tokyo: Iwanami.
— [1986] *The Collected Papers, 1-10*, Tokyo: Iwanami.
National Research Council [1989] *Improving Risk Communication*. Washington, D.C.: National Academies Press, p.21.
Neurath, Otto [1921] *Anti-Spengler*, München: Georg Callway.
— [2011] *The Language of the Global Polis*, Rotterdam: Nai Uitgevers Pub.

Neurath, Otto, Carnap, Rudolf, and Morris, Charles (eds,) [1944] *International Encyclopedia of Unified Science*, Chicago: University of Chicago Press.

Nishida Kitaro [1993/1945] *Last Writings: Nothingness and Religious Worldview*, translated by David Dilworth, Hawaii: University of Hawaii Press.

Nussbaum, Martha [2000] *Women and Human Development: The Capabilities Approach*, Cambridge: Cambridge UP.

— [2006] *Frontiers of Justice: Disability, Nationality Species Membership*, Cambridge, MA, Harvard UP.

Nussbaum, Martha, et al. [1996] *For Love of Country: Debating the Limits of Patriotism*, Boston: Beacon Press.

Ogyū Sorai [1987/1716-36] *Discourse on Politics* (*Seidan* in Japanese), Tokyo: Iwanami.

Ozaki Makoto [2001], *Individuum, Society, Humankind: The Triadic Logic of Species According to Hajime Tanabe*, Leiden: Brill.

Perkins, Franklin [2007] *Leibniz and China: A Commerce of Light*, Cambridge: Cambridge UP.

Piovesana, Gino K. [1997] *Recent Japanese Philosophical Thought 1862-1994: A Survey,* London: Routledge.

Pogge, Thomas (2002) *World Poverty and Human Rights*, Cambridge: Polity Press.

Popper, Karl [1957] *The Poverty of Historicism*, London: Routledge.

— [1984] *Auf der Suche nach einer besseren Welt*, München: Pieper.

Putnam, Robert [1993] *Making Democracy Work: Civic Traditions in Modern Italy*, New Jersey: Princeton UP.

Quine, Willard van Orman [1960] *Word and Object*, Cambridge, MA: MIT Press.

Rawls, John [1971] *A Theory of Justice,* Cambridge, MA: Harvard UP.

— [2005/1993] *Political Liberalism*, New York: Columbia UP.

— [1999] *The Law of Peoples with "The Idea of Public Reason Revisited,"* Cambridge, MA: Harvard UP.

Rice, Daniel F. [1993] *Reinhold Niebuhr and John Dewey: An American Odyssey*, Albany, New York: State University of New York Press.

Ricoeur, Paul [1969] *Le conflit des interpretations: Essais d'hermeneutique*, Paris: Seuil.

Rose, Richard [2012/1986] *The Making of the Atom Bomb*, 25th Anniversary Edition, New York: Simon & Schuster.

Sandel, Michael J. [1982] *Liberalism and the Limits of Justice*, Cambridge: Cambridge UP.

— [1996] *Democracy's Discontent: America in Search of a Public Philosophy*, Cambridge, MA: Harvard UP.

— [2005] *Public Philosophy: Essays on Morality in Politics*, Cambridge, MA: Harvard UP.

Sansom, George Bailey [1962] *The Western World and Japan*, New York: Alfred A. Knopf.

Schad-Seifert, Annette [2003] "Constructing national identities: Asia, Japan and Europe in Fukuzawa Yukichi's theory of civilization," in Stegewerns, Dick (ed.) *Nationalism and Internationalism in Imperial Japan*, London: Routledge, pp. 45-67.

Schelling, Friedrich Wilhelm Joseph [1974/1802] *Vorlesung über die Methode des akademischen Studiums*, Hamburg: Felix Meiner.

Schleiermacher, Friedrich Ernst Daniel [2002/1812-17] *Lectures on Philosophical Ethics*, edited by R. B. Louden, Cambridge: Cambridge UP.

Schnädelbach, Herbert [1984] *Philosophy in Germany 1831-1933*, Cambridge UP.

Schopenhauer, Arthur [1972/1858] *Die Welt als Wille und Vorstellung*, Leipzig: F.A. Brockhaus.

Schütz, Alfred. [1932/1974] *Der sinnhafte Aufbau der sozialen Welt: Eine Einleitung in die verstehende Soziologie*, Frankfurt am Main: Suhrkamp.

Sen, Amartya [1995] *Inequality Reexamined*, Oxford: Oxford UP.

— [1999] *Reason before Identity,* Oxford: Oxford UP.

— [2000] *Development as Freedom*, New York: Anchor Books.

Shionoya, Yuichi (ed.) [2001] *The German Historical School*, London: Routledge.

Spaemann, Robert [1989] *Glück und Wohlwollen: Versuch über Ethik,* Stuttgart: Klett-Cotta.

— [2011] *Nach uns die Kernschmelze: Hybris im atomaren Zeitalter*, Stuttgart: Klett-Cotta.

Spaemann, Robert, and Löw, Reinhard [2005/1981] *Natürliche Ziele: Geschichte und Wiederentdeckung des teleologischen Denkens,* Stuttgart: Klett-Cotta.

Spinoza, Baruch de [1958] *The Political Works*, edited and translated with an introduction and notes by A.G Wernham, Oxford: Clarendon Press.

Stegewerns, Dick [2003] "Yoshino Sakuzo: The isolated figurehead of the Taisho generation," in Stegewerns, Dick (ed.) *Nationalism and Internationalism in Imperial Japan*, London: Routledge, pp. 114-132.

Szpilman, Christopher W. A. [1998] "The Dream of One Asia: Ōkawa Shūmei and Japanese Pan-Asianism," in Fuess, Harald (ed.) *The Japanese Empire in East Asia and Its Postwar Legacy*, München: Iudicium Verlag GmbH, pp. 49-63.

Takagi, Jinzaburō [2000] *Living as a Citizen Scientist* (*Shimin Kagakusha toshite Ikiru* in Japanese) Tokyo: Iwanami.

Takii, Kazuhiro (ed.) [1998] *Lorenz von Steins Arbeiten für Japan*, Frankfurt am Main: Peter Lang.

Tanabe, Hajime [2010/1934-37] *The Logic of the Species*, (*Shu no Ronri* in Japanese) Tokyo: Iwanami.

— [1990/2010/1946] *Philosophy As Metanoetics (Zangedo toshite no Tetsugaku* in Japanese*)*, translated by Takeuchi Yoshinori (Nanzan Studies in Religion and Culture), Oakland: University of California Press on Demand.

— [1975/1947] "Christianity, Marxism and Japanese Buddhism," in *A Collection of Tanabe Hajime* (in Japanese), edited by Nakano Hajimu, Tokyo: Chikuma-shobo, pp. 252-293.

— [1975/1950] "Science, Philosophy and Religion" (Kagaku, Tetsugaku and Shukyo) in *A Collection*, pp. 294-354.

Tanaka, Shōzō [1979/1904-1913] *The Complete Works, Vol. 12* (in Japanese), Tokyo: Iwanami.

— [2004/1879-1903] *The Collected Papers 1* (*Kohdoku to Seiji* in Japanese), Tokyo: Iwanami.

— [2005/1904-1913] *The Collected Papers 2* (*Taninaka no Shiso* in Japanese), Tokyo: Iwanami.

Taylor, Charles [1989] *Sources of the Self: The Making of the Modern Identity,* Cambridge, MA: Harvard UP.
— [2004] *Modern Social Imaginaries*, Durham, North Carolina: Duke UP.
— [2011] *Dilemmas and Connections*, Cambridge, MA: The Belknap Press of Harvard UP.
Taylor, Charles, et al. [1994] *Multiculturalism: Examining the Politics of Recognition*, New Jersey: Princeton UP.
Townsend, Susan C. [2009] *Miki Kiyoshi 1897-1945: Japan's Itinerant Philosopher*, Leiden, Boston: Brill.
Tu Weiming [2006] "The Confucian ethic and the Spirit of East Asian Modernity," in *Cultural Diversity and Transversal Values: East-West Dialogue on Spiritual and Secular Dynamics*, Paris: UNESCO, pp. 7-13.
— [2011] "The Ecological Turn in New Confucian Humanism," in Xinzhong Yao and Weiming Tu (eds.) *Confucian Studies: Critical Concepts in Asian Philosophy, Vol.4,* London: Routledge, pp. 232-258.
Tully, James [2008] *Public Philosophy in a New Key, Vols.1, 2*, Cambridge: Cambridge UP.
Uchida, Yoshihiko [1953] *The Birth of Political Economy* (*Keizaigaku no Seitan* in Japanese) Tokyo: Iwanami.
Ueki, Emori [1990/1879-91] *The Collected Works, Vols.1-5*, Tokyo: Iwanami.
UNESCO [2006] *Cultural Diversity and Transversal Values: East-West Dialogue on Spiritual and Secular Dynamics*, Paris: UNESCO.
U.S. Public Health Service [1995] "Risk Communication: Working with Individuals and Communities to Weigh the Odds," *Prevention Report*, February-March 1995.
von Wright, Georg Henrik [1971], *Explanation and Understanding*, New York, Cornell UP.
Walzer, Michael [1983] *Spheres of Justice: A Defense of Pluralism and Equality,* New York: Basic Books.
— [1994] *Thick and Thin: Moral Argument at Home and Abroad*, Indiana: University of Notre Dame Press.
Walzer, Michael (ed.) [1995] *Toward a Global Civil Society*, Providence: Berghahn Books.
Watsuji, Tetsurō [2007 /1934] *Ethics as a Science of the Human Being* (*Ningen no Gaku toshite no Rinrigaku* in Japanese), Tokyo: Iwanami.
— [1988/1935] *Climate and Culture (Fudo): A Philosophical Study*, Santa Barbara, California: Greenwood Pub Group.
— [1979/1935] *Fudo* (in Japanese), Tokyo: Iwanami.
— [2004/1936-49] *Ethics*, (*Rinrigaku* in Japanese) Tokyo: Iwanami.
— [1996/1936-49] *Rinrigaku: Ethics in Japan*, Translated by Yamamoto Seisaku and Robert E. Carter, Albany: State University of New York Press.
— [1944] "On the National Character of American People," in *Shiso* (in Japanese) February 1944, Tokyo: Iwanami.
— [1982/1950] *Sakoku* (*National Isolation*) (in Japanese), Tokyo: Iwanami.
Weber, Max [1963/1905] "Die protestantische Ethik und der Geist des Kapitalismus," in *Gesammelte Aufsätze zur Religionssoziologie,* Tübingen: Mohr, pp. 17-206.
— [1968a/1904] "Die Objektivität sozialwissenschaftlicher und sozialpolitischer Erken-

ntnis," in *Gesammelte Aufsätze zur Wissenschaftslehre* (hereafter *GAW*), Tubingen: Mohr, pp. 146-216.

— [1968b/1919a] "Wissenschaft als Beruf," in *GAW*, pp. 582-613.

Winch, Peter [1958] *The Idea of a Social Science and Its Relation to Philosophy*, London: Routledge.

Yamawaki, Naoshi [1983] *Die Kontroverse zwischen kritischen Rationalismus und transzendentaler Sprachpragmatik*, Königstein: Hain.

— [1997] "The Philosophical Thought in Japan from 1963 to 1994," in Piovesana, Gino K. (ed.) *Recent Japanese Philosophical Thought, 1862-1996: A Survey*, Richmond, Surrey: Japan Library, pp. 271-287.

— [1999] *Manifesto of a New Trans-disciplinary Social Philosophy* (*Shin Shakai Tetsugaku Sengen* in Japanese), Tokyo: Sobunsya.

— [2001] "Walter Eucken and Wilhelm Röpke: A Reappraisal of Their Economic Thought and the Policy of Ordoliberalism," in Shionoya, Y. (ed.) *The German Historical School: The Historical and Ethical Approach to Economics*, London: Routledge, pp. 188-201.

— [2006] "Toward a Renewal of the Concept 'Wa' (和) for the Culture of Peace," in *Cultural Diversity and Transversal Values: East-West Dialogue on Spiritual and Secular Dynamics*, Paris: UNESCO, pp. 163-166.

— [2007] "Weber's Ideal-type of Development, Politics and Scientific Knowledge," in Mcfalls, Laurence (ed.) *Objectivity Reconsidered*, Toronto: University of Toronto Press, pp. 206-224.

— [2008] *Glocal Public Philosophy: A Vision of Good Societies in the 21st Century* (*Glocal Koukyo Tetsugaku* in Japanese), Tokyo: University of Tokyo Press.

— [2009] "Rehabilitation of Philosophy as Trans-discipline for All Social Sciences," in *Shiso* (*Toransu-disipurin toshiteno Tetsugaku no Fukken* in Japanese), Tokyo: Iwanami, No. 1022, 6. pp. 7-28.

— [2010] "The Idea of Trans-national Public Philosophy as a Comprehensive Trans-discipline for the 21st Century," in *Diogenes* 57 (3), pp. 135-149.

— [2013] "Demokratie und civil society in Japan aus Sicht der *public philosophy*," in Foljanty-Jost, Gesine, and Hüstebeck, Momoyo (eds.) *Bürger und Staat in Japan*, Halle: Universitätsverlag Halle-Wittenberg, pp. 19-40.

Yoshino Sakuzō [1984/1914-1933] *The Collected Papers* (in Japanese), Tokyo: Chuokoronsha.

Yoshioka, Hitoshi [2011] *A Social History of Nuclear Power: Its Japanese Development* (*Genshiryoku no Shakaishi: Sono Nihonteki Tenkai* in Japanese), Tokyo: Asahi Shinbun Publishing.

List of Names